*Her Piece of Sky*

AF673322

# *Her Piece of Sky*

CONTEMPORARY HINDI STORIES

DEEPA AGARWAL
(*Editor*)

zubaan

zubaan

Zubaan
is an imprint of Kali for Women
128b Shahpur Jat
1st floor
New Delhi 110 049
Email: zubaan@gmail.com and zubaanwbooks@vsnl.net
www.zubaanbooks.com

First published by Zubaan, 2011

Copyright © this collection, Zubaan, 2011
© individual story the author, 2011

All rights reserved

10 9 8 7 6 5 4 3 2 1

ISBN: 978 93 81017 06 7

This book is sold subject to the condition that it shall not, by way of trade or otherwise, be lent, resold, hired out, or otherwise circulated without the publisher's prior written consent in any form of binding or cover, other than that in which it is published, and without a similar condition, including this condition, being imposed on the subsequent purchaser, and without limiting the rights under copyright reserved above, no part of this publications may be reproduced, stored in or introduced into a retrieval system, or transmitted in any form or by any means (electronic, mechanical, photocopying, recording or otherwise), without the prior written permission of both the copyright holder and the publisher of this book.

Typeset by: Jojy Philip
Printed at Raj Press, R-3 Inderpuri, New Delhi 110 012

# *Contents*


ACKNOWLEDGEMENTS vii

INTRODUCTION 1
*Deepa Agarwal*

THE CREMATION GROUND 18
*Mannu Bhandari*

THE SECOND ONE 25
*Mridula Garg*

MORASS 46
*Rajee Seth*

THE AGONY OF AN ARTIST 64
*Mamta Kalia*

JAGDAMBA BABU IS COMING TO THE VILLAGE 75
*Chitra Mudgal*

THE DISPOSSESSED 97
*Chandrakanta*

HOMELESS IN THE CANTONMENT 120
*Alpana Mishra*

THERE IS NOTHING ROMANTIC AT ALL 135
*Manisha Kulshreshtha*

UTOPIA 160
*Vandana Rag*

THE HUNT 198
*Pratyaksha*

TRANSFORMATION 212
*Kavita*

CONTRIBUTORS 230

# Acknowledgements

Compiling a collection of stories is not a one woman job—it requires not only the support but the cooperation of many people. First, of all the authors—I'd like to thank all the amazingly talented ladieswho generously contributed their stories and even provided invaluable information about their creative processes,which eased the task of writing the introduction immensely.Then the translators, who put so much effort into rendering the stories into English.A special thanks must go to my friend Chitra Mudgal who shared her invaluable knowledge and even lent books to help me in the selection.Also to Mridula Garg for providing quotes that assessed the development of women's writing in Hindi so precisely. And I have to say that without my editor at Zubaan, Preeti Gill's enthusiasm for this project it would have remained just a gleam in my eye, as it as it had been for many years. Thanks so much, Preeti for having enough faith to take the plunge.

# Introduction

Deepa Agarwal

The genre of the short story has proved to be an effective means of self-expression for women writers in Hindi. Initially, women's stories usually dealt with what were considered feminine concerns – home and the family – or were preoccupied with raising a voice against the oppression of a patriarchal system. It was easier to bring up what could not be said directly at home obliquely, through the medium of fiction, and on a public platform. This kind of protest contributed immensely to the discussion and debate on women's rights and helped women to progress to a self-image beyond those imposed by tradition – the stereotyped ones of wife, daughter, mother, sister or grandmother, rather than individual human beings. But over the decades, women's writing in Hindi has moved beyond the commonly perceived limits of feminine experience. To quote Mridula Garg, one of the most well regarded Hindi writers:

> There is a franker depiction of the larger female experience in women's writing in Hindi. One cannot pinpoint an exact time when the text broke away from expressions of injury. All one can say is that there have always been some women writers, who went beyond injury and delved into the nature of woman and her interaction with society and the universe. The *ardhnarishvara* principle was partly responsible for the progression of feminist writing towards the broader female writing. While feminist writing took half the world as its context, female writing places itself in the context of the entire society or universe, embracing both male and female counterparts; the term of reference progressing from search for identity to social relevance."

This is exactly what many of the stories in this anthology are attempting to do: demonstrate that a woman's 'piece of sky' is not confined merely to the patch that stretches over the inner courtyard. That it reaches way beyond to horizons that are not just imagined but familiar, deeply thought and well explored. In this context, it is worth noting that most of the stories in this collection have been published during the last decade. On the other hand, the two that were published much earlier – Mannu Bhandari's "Shamshaan" and Chitra Mudgal's "Jagdamba Babu Gaon Aa Rahe Hain" also tackle subjects that concern human beings or society as a whole.

Here, I'd like to state that this anthology was not planned with any particular theme in mind. My main intention was to showcase the variety of voices in contemporary women's writing in Hindi and provide newer fare. Some stories by leading names have been translated and anthologised over and over again which means that the reader in English has not had access to many other equally deserving work. Again, many brilliant emerging voices have not been published in English so far. Therefore, along with the work of six well-loved older authors I have included that of five younger writers who are making waves and whose work is exciting, new, complex and multilayered.

The selection of stories for any anthology invariably becomes a daunting task and the line-up will always be incomplete in some way or the other. I have relied mostly on my own reading to shortlist authors. When it came to the final selection, we decided to divide it between the authors, translators and the editor. The authors were asked to suggest stories, the editor then made her choice, and finally the translators made their pick. This was essential, as no translator worth her salt would take on a story that did not call out to her in some way. As it turned out, some of the senior authors selected stories that were personal favourites but for some reason or the other had not been translated or anthologised so far. The younger writers took this as an opportunity to showcase their work, so mostly left the selection to us.

We were also keen to put together a wide range of situations. Hence, in these stories you will find political and social commentary, philosophising on the general human condition, along with individual takes on different kinds of marginalization. Interestingly, despite all the attempts to make it as varied an assortment as possible, on the final reading I found a common note connecting the stories like a luminous thread – a strong sense of irony. This thread, I feel, somehow fits in with the title, which has been adapted from

Rajee Seth's well-known story "Uske Hisse ka Aasmaan" – (His Piece of Sky). Because the same sky stretches over all of us though we may get different views.

To elaborate further: consider, "The Cremation Ground" (Shamshaan), written by legendary writer Mannu Bhandari who is senior-most among the authors featured here. One of her earliest stories, actually her second one, published in the magazine *Kahani,* this philosophical tale consists of a dialogue between two inanimate objects – the cremation ground that is compelled to observe human behaviour during its most vulnerable and emotional moments and the hillock that has the ability to peer into their daily lives and is thus almost cynically aware of the basic nature of humankind. The cremation ground, the place of death, longs to experience emotion, suffer the agonies of love and die for it. However, eventually it is compelled to realize that men's self love or the survival instinct is the force that drives them – far more strongly than any emotional attachment. As the hillock says: "You really are foolish! Don't you understand that a man who loves another person loves life no less? He doesn't survive on the memory, the idea or the spiritual notion of love alone. He loves again and again to experience life to the fullest. Driven by the desire to live, he bears every separation…every agony, because… man loves himself the most."

Mannu Bhandari, who has been associated with the Nai Kahani movement in Hindi literature, says that "Shamshaan" was based on a real life incident and Bhairon Prasad Gupta, who edited *Kahani* then, was highly impressed with her experiment with form, unusual in a new author. Like many authors just starting out, she submitted her work in secret, to avoid the embarrassment of rejection. Interestingly, since she has a name that is common to both sexes, she received many letters from readers that addressed her as "Bhai sahib". She found it heartening, because it made the praise feel sincere, not something handed out to encourage a girl. This was the post-independence era when fiction took inspiration from real life and man-woman relationships were being examined in all honesty, whether it was romance realised, or gone sour – on its own or because of family interference. But as for being listed as an exponent of the Nai Kahani movement, Bhandari says she had no movements in mind when she wrote. She had always enjoyed telling stories, whether it was the tale of a film she had seen narrated to children in her family or any other well-known story, so writing her own felt like the next step.

This kind of satirical comment on the nature of man-woman relationships is echoed in more recent stories like Manisha Kulshreshtha's "Kuch bhi to Rumani Nahin", "There is Nothing Romantic at All". Here the girl protagonist is led astray by the image she has constructed of an author after reading his love stories. As this intriguing narrative unfolds, we discover that in reality she has failed to read her own feelings as well – because more than romantic love, it is her overpowering sexual need that drives her into the man's bedroom. It is telling that she muses in an earlier passage: "In the month of *chaith*, a field of wheat was maturing on my flesh. You could have gone through it. I wanted it. You should have gathered the scattered golden sand of my trembling flesh."

A notable voice from the contemporary generation of writers, Manisha has often startled her readers by bringing issues not often aired to the forefront. Here it is the question of a woman's sexuality – more openly discussed in fiction now and yet, Vanmala, the protagonist must veil her desire under the epithet of love – even to herself. In Bhandari's time, women were taking tentative steps out of the inner courtyard, going to school and college, hesitatingly taking up jobs, the way Bhandari did; something quite revolutionary then. Now, when so many doors and windows have been unbarred, a woman's natural desires can be depicted freely in stories, even though in real life women might balk at boasting of their conquests the way men do, unless it be at a very, very intimate gathering. And something of this attitude is reflected in "There's Nothing Romantic at All."

An overpowering sexual urge drives the protagonist of Pratyaksha's "Shikar" or "The Hunt" as well, a young man obsessed with an older woman. She remains enigmatic, but leaves the man with a memory that will irradiate the dull moments of his life. The author convincingly combines two compelling physical needs – for food and sex – to craft an incredibly sensuous story, in which smell, taste, sight and touch mingle to highly erotic effect. Pratyaksha uses brief, taut sentences to build up the tension that hovers like an overpowering aroma over the story: "All the time, something throbbed like a beating heart, waiting to happen. Waited in the zarda and keema, in the shammi and reshami kebab, in the fragrant spicy betel nut, in the attar and perfume, in the open courtyard, in the veranda, in the clothes left to dry on thin wire hangers, in the enormous legs of the salwars, in the lace edged dupattas, in the narrow legs of the churidaar pyjamas, in bangles and birds, in the doves and the canaries. And one day that waiting placed its lips on my neck below my ears, hot and searing. A wound, burning like a flashing fire..." Here, there is no pretence at romance – it's only the fever of the flesh that pervades the hunt. In both these stories, women boldly assert their sexuality, and the males targeted almost appear to be the victims.

Pratyaksha, who is known for the experimental nature of her work and her sometimes unusual themes, describes herself as a 'garden of 5 senses' on her blog, which seems apt if we take the above story into account. She posts regularly, and has a number of followers. Her stories throb with emotion, sometimes turn philosophical, and cast a haunting spell. Like Manisha, she knows that the contemporary writer must have a strong presence on the internet and makes good use of the possibilities of playing with format in a blog – the white spaces that effectively convey the silences, or sub-text if you prefer to call it, in her stories. In that sense she lives the times, though this particular story is in a sense timeless.

Romance or desire, turns perverse in Vandana Rag's "Utopia". Atchyutanand Gosain, the brutish lover, is driven not only by his religious fanaticism but also his obsession for a young Muslim girl, Najjo, a former playmate whom he tormented as a boy. A fruit-seller's son, Gosain intriguingly sees people as fruit and is sometimes overcome by the urge to slice them through. The red pomegranates in Najjo's face torment him to madness. Rag skilfully builds up an image of the insanity burgeoning within a typical low-level fundamentalist like Gosain, besides portraying the restlessness of a directionless young man, so efficiently channelled by a politician to horrific effect. In this story of communal strife it is the mother, Ammi, who cannot find safety for her child in the new intolerant environment she cannot understand, despite all her efforts to exercise the utmost caution.

Vandana's vision of this utopia is searing, and yet there is a weary sense of *déjà vu*. It reminds you of the gory scenes that numb you while channel surfing, those tirades by the guardians of our culture who annihilate while claiming to protect. The viciousness with which the ordinary dreams of an ordinary mother and daughter are decimated because they come in the way of a larger, cynically amoral scheme of power, is what we encounter in newspaper headlines every day. The difference is that reportage insinuates a cushioning distance, while the story heightens the horror by drawing you in. A student of history, Vandana's first short story collection has just come out. Passionate protest against injustice and an examination of the anomalies in our system mark her work.

Najjo's Ammi tries to make sense of the new bewildering order, but Laspandit in Chandrakanta's wrenching "Sharanagat Deenarth", "The Dispossessed" refuses to read the signs of the times till it is too late. Set amidst the turmoil raging in Kashmir, this is another story of a woman abducted as spoils of war in the relentless battle between communities. Jaya is a random target though, unlike Najjo. And Jaya in the end proves to be the catalyst that drives home the bitterest lesson in his life for Laspandit – that the mantras he chanted with such attention to perfection were totally ineffective. There is no protector for those seeking refuge, even among their own tormented community. His pride in his profession, performing rituals according to proper form, not chanting 'Om-yom' like lesser pandits is cruelly trampled upon by his daughter's fate.

One of the senior writers in this anthology, Chandrakanta, began publishing in the seventies. Like many women authors, she depicts the plight of disadvantaged people and women. Much of her work is set in her native Kashmir, discusses its contemporary problems, or showcases its rich culture. For her "literature is a parallel history of time, but at the same time, it probes deeply into the system, questions it, and tries to find answers". Thus Chandrakanta uses fictional situations to interrogate the systemic failure that overturned an entire culture and highlights the trauma of the dispossessed.

Chitra Mudgal's "Jagdamba Babu Gaon Aa Rahe Hain" "Jagdamba Babu is Coming to the Village" offers political commentary of a different kind, but no less scathing. Here again it is the naïve who are the victims. The hapless Sukhan Bhauji is overwhelmed by Thakur Sumer Singh's benevolence; little realising that she's just a pawn in a much larger game. Political cynicism is as brutally outlined in this story as well. Aspiring leaders do not seem to possess even the barest vestige of a conscience – whether it is Thakur Sumer Singh or Shri Ram Mohan in "Utopia". Sumer Singh's calm statement makes this clear when he takes away the invalid cart publicly gifted to Sukhan Bhauji's disabled son: 'Then he turned to Sukhan Bhauji who stood there trembling, trying to contain the cry that buffeted back and forth between her belly and her throat, "If anyone asks...say it was stolen." '

Chitra Mudgal lays bare the ruthless game being played in the mofussil towns of the country with the keen perception of a sharp-sighted observer of our contemporary reality. Though this story was first published in the 1980s, its relevance still endures. A former trade unionist and an activist for women's rights, Mudgal rebelled against the system early in life when she defied her father to marry out of caste. The feudal structure she depicts is one familiar to her from childhood and she has explored its excesses in other stories too. Mudgal, like Bhandari, picks up her stories from real life and believes that the solid foundation of experience is essential for effective writing. As she said in an interview: "Writers today need to go among people to understand them so as to create more life-like characters that tug at the reader's heart. Only then will the purpose of writing be served."

It is a point worth noting too, that all the stories are set in small towns, bastis and villages, what is often defined as 'Bharat' rather than metropolitan cities.

Mamta Kalia is a somewhat different kind of observer in "The Agony of an Artiste", "Ek Rangkarmi ki Udaasi". In this story of Mishraji, a has-been theatre director, the writer turns a somewhat humorous, though affectionate eye on a man living in a make-believe world. It is an ironical comment on the fickleness of fortune and a man's inability to adapt to his changed situation. She writes: "Old stories are like chronic aches, lingering, lovable, yet incurable. What was there to talk about in the present?" Only the glorious past resonates within him, the failed present is only to be denigrated. The most telling statement comes at the end, when the editor of a new theatre journal requests him to reduce the word length of the article on the history of theatre he has been writing with such enthusiasm and he tears up the piece in a fury. This is the second story that ends with the destruction of a creative work but something in the deceptively easy manner in which Mamta Kalia delineates this tragedy of the ordinary human condition adds a deeply poignant note. Somewhere, each one of us has experienced Mishraji's agony – maybe in a different degree – the nostalgia that will not allow us to live fully in the present. 'He slumped on the divan and said, "Just wait, some day I'll put up a new play, even if it's with a small troupe. Khuda hafiz."'

Kalia, a bilingual writer, is one of the veterans featured in this collection. She began writing in the early '70s when women writers were beginning to make an impact in the world of Hindi literature. She outlined small, domestic struggles in her work and laid emphasis on the significance of women's contribution in every sphere of life. Her novel *Beghar*, a narrative of alienation, aptly captured the mood of the '70s – disillusionment. The romantic Nehruvian era in politics was over. People were becoming disenchanted – independence had not ushered in the utopia everyone had dreamed of. Corruption had not yet reached monstrous dimensions but was making its presence felt in different fields. Thus a kind of cynicism had replaced the earnestness of the '50s and the youthful zest of the '60s, which was reflected in the literature of the decade.

The predicament of the other woman has always been a fascinating topic for writers. Mridula Garg provides this tale with a unique twist in "Vo Doosri", "The Second One". Her grandfather's second wife is an enigma to the young narrator. A woman who has willingly allowed herself to be sidelined, hailing as she does from the randiyon ka mohalla – the locality where prostitutes live, from where she has picked up the art that sets her apart from the respectable ones, the art of singing ghazals in a rich, throbbing voice. It is as if her husband had wilfully chosen her to entertain him within the decent limits of his own home. And yet, she is not considered fit to bring up her own children. The second one is dehumanised to the extent that when she loses the child conceived at a late age, no one sympathises – rather, they are relieved. At this point she abandons her art, silences her resonating voice. In the end, the startling revelation about the first wife, who has almost been deified, sums up the hypocrisy prevalent in so called 'decent' families. To quote: "It was not their fault," said Ma to me, "when someone dies, he or she ceases to be a person and becomes the protagonist of a play. As if dying was everything and the person counted for nothing."

Mridula Garg is a writer who has always set her own boundaries. According to eminent writer Manohar Shyam Joshi: "Mridula does not belong to any tradition, a word so dear to Hindi critics. She has a world view and style of her own, which steers clear of Marxist doctrine, mythological throwback, feminist discourse, regional culture fix, in short, of all possible stereotypes." She horrified critics with the untrammelled sexuality of her women characters and was actually arrested on charges of obscenity for her novel *Chitta-cobra* (Cobra–self) in 1980. Brought up in a liberal family where girls were encouraged to read, three among her five sisters became writers. Mridula does not hesitate to experiment and uninhibitedly tackles a variety of themes in her writing. Her canvas ranges from family to public life, from the personal to the political.

Several stories use unusual family situations to explore more wide-ranging issues. In Kavita Rakesh's thought provoking "Ulatbansi" or "Transformation", Apoorva, the protagonist finds herself in a strange dilemma. Her widowed mother, more or less abandoned by her brothers, has decided to get remarried. The brothers and their wives are appalled and she and her young niece are the only ones who support her. And yet, as she performs the 'vidai' for her mother she faces another quandary. Her insensitive husband has given her an ultimatum – she is not to return home if she stays back to attend the mother's marriage. As she searches for him at the railway station, the wrenching thought seizes her: "The keys Ma gave me jangle in my purse in response...why did she give these to me? Had she understood what was going on...and still...? Will I have to make my way back to that locked room...to her loneliness? Like the sun and moon, had Ma and I exchanged roles?"

Women may have stepped out of the inner courtyard but their struggle has acquired new dimensions in the twenty-first century. A young writer who has received acclaim for bringing poignant focus on the contemporary dilemmas women are facing, Kavita is carving her own niche among the women writers of today. While Mridula Garg uncovered the stifling hold of the joint family in the seventies, Kavita examines the problems posed by the nuclear family lifestyle in this subtly crafted story. In both situations women bear the brunt. Kavita says: "Writing is a kind of torment for me, a restlessness to find myself...unpeel the layers of my being...I exist, I am a woman, how can I deny the extent of my power, and if I don't voice my sorrow, my pain, who will?"

"Chhavani mein Beghar", "Homeless in the Cantonment" and "Daldal", "Morass" both deal with problems faced by army wives but address two very different issues. While "Morass" is the tale of a woman with a husband who cannot pull himself free from the quagmire of his male ego, "Homeless" is an indictment of the heartlessness of the military bureaucracy that callously uproots women whose husbands are serving on the front from their homes. While in a sense it is the forces of patriarchy that can be said to be at play here, because the administration only provides proper accommodation to officers reunited with their families, ironically, this unjust system serves to empower the separated wives as they learn to fend for themselves. Mishra's complex and exquisitely crafted story is rich with layers of meaning. Meenu, who learns to think of herself as Mrs Kumar when her husband receives a promotion, observes the many facets of patriotism: "The soap bar is wrapped in the tricolour. The more patriotic you are the more soap bars you will buy. A major automobile manufacturer has come out with a new range of cars in the different colours of the national flag...Outside the Red Fort a police jawan has taken his officer hostage. Terrorists have created a minefield stretching from the native village to Delhi. People are walking on it. Those who matter, fly... The air is heavy with the sound of a worldwide dirge. The newspapers and magazines are busy extracting contributions in the names of the martyrs from the public... the handsome captain who used to play the mouth organ has become a martyr and a symbol of bravery. A young lieutenant who made sketches of Param Veer Chakra-winning martyrs has joined their ranks. He has been wiped out along with his art." Need we say more?

An army wife, Mishra conveys an insider's perspective in this hard-hitting story. This gifted author's work occupies a special place in the ranks of contemporary writers. She has brought another dimension to women's fight for space, for dignity in her existence by highlighting situations that are often ignored. As someone has said, the new generation of writers are not saviours or reformers; they turn such a searing gaze on reality and compel us to re-examine worn out, established values. Mishra's lyrical sentences resonate with meaning, her characters are often engaged in a dialogue with themselves, which may haunt or occasionally startle the reader. She makes an impact by understating things rather than dramatising them. She exposes the indifference of authority to real problems in her other writing too, like her satire on academic life *Tamasha* (Spectacle), or prejudice in her tongue-in-cheek tale of unequal love in the animal world *Jimmy ke Sapne* (Jimmy's Dreams).

Aartee in "Morass" is engaged in a different struggle – to find suitable employment for her disabled husband. He, on the other hand, is bent on thwarting all her attempts to rehabilitate him, trapped as he is in the morass of distrust about her relationship with her employer. Beneath the cloak of suspicion we can glimpse the male chauvinism that compels a man to feel demeaned by his wife's honest efforts. Veteran writer Seth depicts the back and forth movement of Aratee's struggle to maintain harmony, despite the "dry rot" of her married life, with great sensitivity. And in this story too, we get the feeling that in the end it is Aratee who has gained from this battle despite the lack of understanding and empathy that surrounds her. As the author says at the end: "But she said nothing. Just asked for the strength to gather the four corners of her house that were threatening to fly apart into her hands. Asked it of herself. Only of herself." It is almost as if through her superhuman efforts to maintain an accord with the disparate spaces of home and work, to provide and nurture while holding on to her own soul, she has achieved the status of the goddess that is often ascribed to Indian women.

Rajee Seth has lived the conflict between family duties and their creative needs. Like many Indian women she let her muse find voice only when an overpowering angst could not be contained any longer. She completed her studies and began writing rather late in life. However, her incisive examination of ordinary lives and the grinding misery of the daily struggle soon established her as a strong voice amongst women writers of her generation. Rajee depicts the ambivalence women experience – the painful negotiations for breathing space, the clash between the roles of homemaker and breadwinner with deep perception and unveils human foibles with the merciless vision of a seasoned observer of the dance of life. Of her own work she states that her stories examine the effects of events rather the events themselves, and that sometimes characters, situations burst on her consciousness in their entirety, with such intensity that often her first draft turns out to be the best.

So many women, so many stories, challenges, protests and enquiry. The short story as conceived by women continues to widen its range, seeks new frontiers to conquer even as it pauses on the way to peer beneath surfaces left unplumbed. To quote Mridula Garg again – 'Women writers have moved beyond immanence and reached transcendence; as they take responsibility for themselves and choose freedom in action as well as in writing.' The keywords here are responsibility and freedom. By making this choice women writers are not only embracing a path that carries them to new planes of existence but also opening up fresh vistas for readers, even though they be reluctant messiahs.

# The Cremation Ground

*Mannu Bhandari*

It must have been around ten at night. At one end of the cremation ground, spreading out his bedding with carefree ease, the dom belted out a couplet of Kabir's: *Jehi ghat prem na sancharay, soi ghat jaan masaan* (The heart that is devoid of love is like the cremation ground)!

The cremation ground was overcome with emotion. Sighing deeply, it said to the hillock that stood next to it, "The more I love man, the more he hates me. No man wishes to see my face while he is alive. But the truth is I am not that terrible. I am the one who offers him refuge when the world is no longer prepared to keep him for even one day. For me, all men are the same: young and old, poor and rich. But what use is it? I don't possess that capacity for love that is man's greatest treasure. The light of love, which might have earned me a place in his heart doesn't glow in mine. I don't know why God has treated me so unjustly."

The hillock, which stood between the town and the cremation ground, smiled. Its mocking smile stung the cremation ground.

It asked, "Don't you ever wish that, like man, you too had a tender heart, pulsating with the longing to sacrifice his life for his beloved? Sometimes, when the winds that blow from faraway lands recount the tales of the glorious love of Laila-Majnoon and Shireen-Farhad, believe me, this desire consumes me. Oh! If I could be Majnoon too and give up my life, overcome by the agony of my separation from Laila. I would spread myself like a carpet on my beloved's path, as I wait for her. The dark, heavy, monsoon clouds would stir up an unbearable ache in my heart and dusky spring evenings would transform into an endless yearning. My beloved's life would be my whole existence, and her death, my death. But what can I do? God created me as a cremation ground that has no love or passion in its heart, no feelings, no warmth, just the flames of funeral pyres burning day and night."

The hillock that kept one eye on the cremation ground and the other on the town and its inhabitants, inquired, "Do you really have such a great wish to be human? "

"Wish? I could sacrifice a hundred lives such as mine to possess a heart with a capacity to love, like man."

The hillock smiled.

Suddenly, piteous wails wrenched the heart of the cremation ground. A small group had arrived, bearing a corpse. A handsome young man was weeping bitterly, as if he had been deprived of all that was precious to him. The corpse was placed on the ground. It was his wife they had brought to cremate here. The young man's grief pierced the cremation ground's heart. The group completed the rituals and somehow managed to calm the bereaved man and take him home. The cremation ground kept thinking – how deeply he must have loved his wife. I wish I too could love someone like that!

The next evening, in the dim light of dusk, the cremation ground saw the young man again. His face was unrecognizable – it was as if he had aged overnight. His eyes were swollen and bloodshot. Staggering like a madman, he gathered up his wife's ashes. Tears streamed down his cheeks, his frame was racked with sobs. Then he seemed to lose all control and banging his head wildly, shrieked, "Where have you gone Sukeshi? Remember, you vowed that you would stay with me all my life? It's only been two years and you have gone, leaving me all alone. I can't live without you. Take me with you or I will have to find a way to come to you. Without you, my life has no meaning, no sense, no pleasure – you were my whole being, my inspiration. What reason do I have to exist now? Call me to yourself Sukeshi, I can't live without you, I can't, there's no way...."

Beating his head, the young man wailed and lamented. The voiceless cremation ground watched the scene with its arid, stony eyes, and its desire to be human, to love, and to die yearning for one's beloved, like this young man, grew. It kept thinking, oh, if only I could love somebody so – with all my heart and soul!

Standing next to it, the hillock kept smiling.

Finally, done with weeping, the young man departed, but

his tears continued to scorch the heart of the cremation ground like hot irons.

It said to the hillock, "This man's grief has wrung my heart through and through. Though many such men come here everyday, there was something in this particular man's pain and his anguish that I will never forget. Mark my words; this young man will not live long. He has reduced his frame to half in just one day of mourning. How can he survive? He will definitely die of grief. I too, hope that he lays his head on my lap soon so that I can unite the two lovers."

The next day the cremation ground waited for the young man's arrival on a bier, but his corpse did not appear. Yes, around dusk the young man did turn up himself to give vent to his terrible grief. This routine continued for a few days. Then the young man stopped coming. But the cremation ground could not forget him. It would examine each and every corpse eagerly and become a little crest-fallen when he did not find him.

One day it asked the hillock, "You can peer into each nook and cranny of the town, can you tell me how that young man is faring?"

The hillock smiled, "No."

The cremation ground continued, "Something inside me keeps insisting that he has killed himself. Perhaps he drowned himself, or used some such method to end his life that his corpse cannot reach me. How I wish I could unite him with his beloved!"

The hillock asked, "You do believe he is dead?"

The cremation ground was irritated. "You are truly made

of stone. No one whose heart has been pierced by the pain of love can survive such a loss."

The hillock simply smiled.

Days passed. Watching people weep for their departed loved ones, the cremation ground became even more convinced of man's capacity for love. It became almost a routine: the cremation ground sang paeans to this divine quality in human beings, the hillock just smiled.

Three years passed this way. These three long years could not erase the memory of the young man's grief from the cremation ground's mind. It often talked about him; of the tears he had shed for his beloved, of the inimitable devotion that certainly must have forced him to commit suicide. It talked of the young man's poignant wails that still wrung its heart.

Then one day, its heart quaked hearing a familiar voice raised in pitiful shrieks. It saw the same handsome young man appear with a small crowd of mourners carrying a bier. The cremation ground thought, he's still alive. Now what fresh calamity could have befallen the unfortunate soul this time?

But from the conversation of the mourners it soon became clear that this particular deceased too, had been his wife. Everyone seemed to be saying the same thing, "This poor fellow is not destined for marital bliss, or why would he lose two wives within five years? To think he is so young..."

On this day too, the young man's wails were heart-rending in the extreme, his shrieks tore at the heart, and his tears were just as hot and burning. He didn't look any different from what he had the first time. The mourners managed to console him somehow, and took him home.

The cremation ground's faith in the sublimity of man's love was somewhat shaken. In the evening the young man arrived again, and rolling in the ashes of his departed wife, wept, "Not even in my dreams could I have imagined you would leave me like this. Why, oh why did you become my companion if you were going to abandon me half way? How will I live without you? With your sweet smile, in a single day you wiped off the pain of Sukeshi's separation. I was completely yours, heart and soul. You were my life. How will this lifeless body survive now? I can't bear to remain in this world anymore. Oh, take me with you. Sukeshi was obedient and subservient. Maybe that is why I didn't feel her absence so much; but you were my true companion, we were two bodies with a single soul. What is a body without its soul?"

The young man continued to visit the cremation ground, wail for hours and go away. There was such power in his tears, such truth in his wailing that the slight crack of doubt that had developed in the cremation ground's belief filled up. Once again it began to wait for the young man's corpse to appear. It was convinced that this time the trauma would surely end his life. It longed to unite the young man and his wife forever. But the young man's bier never arrived. The cremation ground's wish remained unfulfilled. The routine continued to repeat itself. Each day numerous corpses were burnt, men wept, the cremation ground extolled the divineness of human love and the hillock smiled. There was one difference though – the cremation ground's voice had less conviction now and the hillock's smile became broader and more unambiguous. It thought, perhaps the young man had married her for some compelling reason, without actually loving her.

It was disillusioned when it again heard his cries. The young man's wails were just as heart-rending, his shrieks just as blood curdling, even his tears just as corrosive. He didn't look any different from the first time. His words were the same too, the only difference being, his third wife appeared to have been the best of the three. He declared he had known true love only with her, that his love for the first two women had been the mere callowness of youth. The first one had been a follower, the second one a companion but this last one was his guide, without whom he could not take a single step. Now he would have to die, he couldn't live even one day without her. The same old words, the same laments, the same weeping – as if this had no connection with his real sentiments and he were repeating it like a lesson, something learnt by rote.

Watching this scene, the cremation ground that had treasured the belief that human love was truly sublime, turned to stone. It watched the goings on, bewildered and speechless. Then a question seemed to rear up in its dazed eyes.

The hillock was filled with pity, observing its confusion. It said, "You really are foolish! Don't you understand that a man who loves another person loves life no less? He doesn't survive on the memory, the idea or the spiritual notion of love alone. He loves again and again to experience life to the fullest. Driven by the desire to live, he bears every separation... every agony, because... man loves himself the most."

*Translated by Madhu B. Joshi*

# *The Second One*

*Mridula Garg*

There are at least three women in every human being's life. Their mother and two grandmothers, nani and dadi. It was my misfortune that I never knew my nani or dadi. Both of them died before my parents got married. My existence remained unacknowledged by them.

Nana did not remarry, so nani's place was taken by her memories. Ma never tired of telling me stories about her. The mystique of her persona was kept alive for me. But did I have a kink in my brain! It was dadi I thought of even as I listened to the stories about nani. Dadi, whom even my father had never known, let alone my mother. She had died immediately after giving birth to my father. By the time my mother came into his life, the second one had been there for ages. You can easily guess that dada had remarried before the year was out, after his wife's death. The only dadi I knew was the second one.

No, we did not call her the second one. It was she, who by constantly referring to the deceased dadi as the first one established herself as the second one. On the rare occasions, when Ma shifted from nani to dadi, it was the second one she talked about. As far as the first one was concerned, it was the second one who had told her whatever little she knew about her.

Ma said that when she came to her in-law's house as a bride, she was welcomed ceremonially, not by her mother-in-law but by the mother-in-law's older sister-in-law, that is my father's tai. The aunt had sighed long and deep as she helped Ma cross the threshold and said, "How happy *she* would have been, if *she* were here today! Not that this one isn't...*Arre o chhoti*..."

The high note of a ghazal splintered and faded away. Ma had picked up its throbbing pulse right at the entrance of the house but it had not crossed her mind that it could be connected to her mother-in-law. Now she saw a woman, who was not motherly in any way, rise from the floor with an uneasy air of leaving something half done. Ma's stand-in mother-in-law declared, "Bahu, now this one is your mother-in-law."

The woman made no move to come close or ask Ma to come to her. She raised her hand in blessing and intoned, "*Doodhon nahao, pooton phalo*" – may you prosper and bear many sons, then added, "If the first one had been here, she would have been so happy!" Having said her piece, she sank back on the floor and pulled the harmonium towards her to resume the lyric. The sensuous notes of the ghazal rose and encircled them, captivating the whole room. The longing expressed by the husky but melodious timbre of her voice invoked the sensual aura of a performance by a courtesan. Ma felt awkward and uncertain as she stood and gazed at her. It never crossed her mind to go and touch her feet. Not that tai gave her much time. She hustled her to the other end of the room to complete the ceremonies.

That woman continued with her full-throated song, tackling the high notes with gravelled sweetness. The gaggle of women who surrounded her did not make any attempt to get up and approach the bride. Tai pointed to one and said, "That one in the gold-threaded green sari is my sister's daughter, Bitto, like my own daughter, you know." But she did not call her over. Bitto sat with a dholki but she was no longer playing it. Perhaps the ghazal had moved to a realm quite beyond her limited skill. She might tap her fingers in accompaniment afterwards...perhaps...

"The women will be here soon for the munh dikhayi ceremony. You better sit down." Tai asked Ma to sit on a low stool. She did, but her attention remained riveted to the ghazal, which was fast approaching its climax. She was so absorbed in it that she felt no anxiety about being 'seen' by the women or their beady-eyed inspection and caustic comments.

Even now Ma seemed captivated by the memory, as she narrated the story. "I did not understand then," she said, "why was it so hard to decide if the husky voice, weaving a lush web around them was feminine or masculine. I knew it was mesmerizing but for whom; a man or a woman? I know now that sensual appeal is beyond these labels, I didn't then."

Just then a true-blue male voice had boomed, "Tell her to keep it down."

The woman did not stop singing instantly. It just could not be done on that note. But a natural break must have occurred soon in the lyric, because the words, added softy by the male voice, were heard by everyone. "After all she is from a randiyon ka mohalla..."

The phrase was drowned in collective, raucous male laughter. The speaker too sounded more jocular than indignant. She stopped singing and pushed the harmonium aside but she did not look embarrassed or insulted. Ma watched her fascinated, as a knowing half-smile played on her lips, as if she had once again heard a well-worn flirtatious phrase. Poor Ma was embarrassed enough for both of them. Her face grew hot and beads of sweat rolled down her forehead. Her mother-in-law could not but notice it. She laughed and said, "That's what he says over and over again... the same old words...."

The village women began to arrive. There was not one of them, who failed to say, "If *she* were here today, *she* would have been so happy..."

The second one laughed and added, "The first one may not be here but jethaniji is." When she had repeated it four or five times, tai finally said, "So are you, chhoti."

"Sure," she tinkled, "I'm always here in place of the first one."

Ma had found it all rather strange. Later, the second one's stories helped her to unravel some of the knots.

Ma's greatest curiosity lay in the phrase, randiyon ka mohalla. But there was no way she could utter the words.

All she could do was to wait for the second one to bring it up. She did not have to wait long. The second one had no qualms about talking about it. Reticence was not part of her nature.

"I was a girl from a poor family, even if an only child. Our house was in one of the back lanes of the randiyon ka mohalla. Such pulsating ghazals floated around us when the prostitutes performed in the evenings that I would almost swoon. Should I tell you something, bibi? Don't tell jethaniji. We had a temple too near our house. They sang religious songs there, morning and evening. The bhajans were very well sung but not a patch on the ghazals…you could not even begin to compare the two. What can I tell you about the ghazals? Ah, the rhythm, the lyrics, the melody…enough to compel your feet to break into dance! But I did not dance. All that I did was to sing to myself, imitating them. What strong, luscious voices they had, the women across the street. I heard them entranced, absorbing each word till I could hit the high notes to match theirs. By my good fortune, my mother was hard of hearing. The good soul barely heard them, how could she hear poor me? She did not know to what pitch my voice had risen. My father was equally clueless but for a different reason. He was away from home most of the time, in a futile bid to earn two square meals. He might have put a stop to my singing, had he heard me. I was not so foolish as to do my riyaz when he was home. Riyaz! What next!" She dissolved into laughter as she said "riyaz" as if surprised at her own audacity, then clarified after a belly laugh, "Practice bibi, practice." She stopped her narration and busied herself with the harmonium but took up the threads of the story again after a few days.

"After the first one was gone, your father- in-law, bauji, set about looking for a new wife. When he reached our humble quarters, my extreme foolishness was revealed to everyone. When bauji told my father he wanted to remarry for the sake of his children, so needed a bride from a poor family, my father thought salvation was at hand. As for me, I almost capsized the boat... lucky we managed to stay afloat."

Bauji told us that he had heard that I could sing, so he wanted to hear me. I wondered where he got the information. Later I realized, of course, if the women's voices from across the street could reach my house, mine would have reached their houses and bauji...!

Well, that came later. That day as soon as he asked me to sing, I launched into a sonorous ghazal, singing it at a pitch that sent everyone into shock. My notes actually had a feverish quality. You know, bibi, when nervous, even an experienced rider is either unable to move or forgets to rein in the horse. So there I was galloping away...my father's heartbeat nearly stopped when he heard me sing with such abandon. But bauji laughed saying, 'After all, she is from the randiyon ka mohalla. Never mind, she will learn.'

"Learn what? I wondered, learn to lower my voice, or learn not to sing ghazals? My father must have thought he meant the latter. He gave me a real piece of his mind after bauji left but did not berate me for long. After all, bauji had not walked away from the match. My mother though, I must say, was even crazier than I. She said happily, 'Our son-in-law is a rasik, a real connoisseur. He was in a trance listening to her sing!'

"It's not that I haven't tried to keep my voice down, bibi. I have. Haven't I been scolded by bauji often enough. He is forever saying, there was the first one, so well-bred, delicate and refined and here you are, ill-bred, big-boned, and... Not just bauji, everyone says so. There was the first one and there is this one. That's why bauji handed over all his four sons to jethaniji – two of the first one and two of mine. They needed to be brought up properly, you see. They are all she has, anyway; fate did not grant her any children of her own. Her sister's child is there, but a daughter. You have to grant that jethaniji is truly just and fair. She might say twenty times a day that her sister's daughter is like her own, but she always gives more importance to the boys, her nephews. All four of them went to the best schools and colleges. The two younger ones are still studying, the eldest has a good job in the city and this one, your husband, will get one too, sooner or later. She has never denied them their due. Jethji is no different from his younger brother, your bauji. You know that bauji can't bear daughters. He always says, 'Thank God for not giving me any daughters.' If a daughter of his was to sing like me, he would have wrung her neck. So why didn't he wring mine? Go on ask, bibi, I have the answer. He might tell me a thousand times to keep my voice down but he can't help thirsting after... the ghazals. Every now and then, he orders me imperiously, 'You from the randiyon ka mohalla, let me hear one of your throbbing ghazals.'"

Ma was enthralled as she listened, but also fearful. Should she try to get closer to her, she wondered? It was impossible to look upon her or imagine her as a mother-in-law. It was tai who was a mother-in-law, prim and proper, boring and comforting. When Ma was with tai, my father sometimes joined them but he gave them a wide berth if she was with the second one. Ma felt very curious about her real mother-in-law, so she asked my father what she was like.

"I don't know, I never saw her," he replied coldly. The ensuing silence stretched till she felt both of them had aged considerably in that time.

My mother was a lawyer's daughter, afflicted with the urge to investigate puzzles till she found a solution. She surmised that her husband had not forgiven his mother for dying soon after giving birth to him. But what about the second one, why was he equally cold when she asked him about her? Ma told him that she couldn't understand the second one. Should she spend more time with her? After all, she was her mother-in-law. "She is what she is," he said, and the silence between them stretched till she felt both of them had grown older than the second one's rasik husband at least. His silence stoked Ma's curiosity. She realized that if she wanted to know anything about the first one, she would have to tap the second one.

If she asked anyone in the village including the tai about the first one, they tended to describe her as a combination of a goddess and a celestial beauty. My Ma, a lawyer's argumentative daughter, heard nothing but a tissue of lies in their accounts. "It was not their fault," said Ma to me, "when someone dies, he or she ceases to be a person and becomes the protagonist of a play. As if dying was everything and the person counted for nothing." The second one was the only one for whom the first one was not dead. She was always beside her, in flesh and blood, towering above her. She may not have seen her, but had the living proof of her being a female, in her two sons. She could glimpse her face in their faces. Her sterling qualities were extolled endlessly by the people in the village, especially in comparison to her, the second one. She was not so gullible as to swallow it wholesale. But she did conclude that the first one was poles apart from her. It was not painful to try and imagine someone, who was her opposite; in fact it held a certain fascination. She managed to create a fairly credible flesh and blood image of her.

I am certain that if Ma had persisted, she could have persuaded the second one to give her a fuller description of the first and in the bargain, partly of herself. But Ma chickened out. Whether it was the effort involved or the fear of discovering forbidden areas, which made her retreat, I can't say. She did confess that she found the company of the second one as scary as it was exciting.

As the day's food was being placed on the fire to cook, the second one would spread out the game of chaupad and say, "Come bibi, let's play a few rounds." Ma would hesitate and ask, "What about the cooking?" "Jethaniji will take care of it," the second one would remark casually. Ma would be in two minds but then would invariably hear tai call, "Bahurani! Come here..." Whenever she saw Ma spending too much time with the second one, Tai was sure to find some chore for her, summoning her with a loving, "Bahurani!" Ma would run to do her duty. She never forgot to tell the second one that she'd be back soon but by the time she got back, she found the second one had moved on to something else.

At other times she'd say, "Come, I'll teach you to play the tabla. You play and I'll sing. The harmonium is not enough by itself; it can provide the scale but not the beat. Or would you prefer to learn a ghazal?" Horror would turn Ma speechless. "Tai is calling me," she'd say, and make a run for it.

Whatever conversation they managed to have was while tracing patterns on saris in preparation for embroidering them.

The story was not narrated in one sitting but in bits and pieces over many days. It began on the day they got some fine voile for saris in lovely colours from the city, just before the spring festival of basant panchami. The second one spread out a yellow length and said to Ma, "I've heard you're good at tracing patterns. Trace some flowers on this sari. I'll fill in the threads or ask Bitto to do it. She's quite neat with embroidery but not everyone can draw. I'd say it requires as much talent as singing or playing. Anyway I'm not asking you to sketch portraits, just a few flowers and leaves. I know you can do that much." Ma traced some flowery patterns carefully on the voile. But whether the second one or Bitto filled them up, she did not know. She never saw them do it. The second one was always tinkering with the harmonium or playing chaupad.

Ma did not stay in the village for long. She'd known all along that my father would get a job in the city. But she didn't expect it to happen within four months. As the time to leave the village approached, she felt an urgency to get closer to the second one to find out more about the first one.

But things took such an unexpected turn that all her schemes went awry. She discovered that she was pregnant. Before she could announce it with a proper show of modesty and enjoy extra attention from tai, they were all stunned by a shocking piece of news. The second one was also pregnant! The family forgot all about celebrating Ma's good news and plunged into deep embarrassment over the second one's unexpected pregnancy. No one more than my grandfather, the second one's rasik bauji! To follow in the footsteps of the son at his age! This was not a ghazal, which could be laid at door of the randiyon ka mohalla and leave him blameless. He could barely face my father till he left for the city. The second one suffered from no such shame. She declared her joy openly before everybody. As if it weren't Ma but she, who was pregnant for the first time. Ma took her transgression to heart. She couldn't bring herself to talk civilly to her.

The only saving grace was that when my father moved to the city, nobody objected to Ma going with him. The second one's pregnancy cast such a pall of shame that tai herself provided the perfect excuse. Since bahu had a delicate constitution, she said, she should have her baby in the hospital under proper medical care, in the city and not in the village. "We've suffered bereavement once, we can't be too careful now," she added. Nobody cared to ask her, what about the second one? Tai had the answer ready anyway. It was not her first time; she had two normal deliveries earlier. The second one – she was not interested in Ma or anyone else. She was in such a haze of delight over her third pregnancy that she could not think of any ill befalling her.

Nine months went by and two girls were born at two different locations. My bua, the second one's daughter and I. I'm alive and kicking till today but my bua lived only for a few hours. Everyone took refuge in the she-was-God's-own-beloved adage, passing the sole responsibility to God, secretly heaving sighs of relief at her death. The second one was so scarred by the tragedy that she was never quite herself again. She took refuge in silence after saying, "There was the first one, she died but her child survived and here am I! I have killed my child and I am alive!"

Whatever Ma might have told me about the second one – I had seen her only as an old woman. Dada seemed comparatively younger. The idea of her singing ghazals was unthinkable for me. I don't think, I had ever heard her hum even a bhajan. In fact I don't remember hearing her sing, laugh or talk at all. All I ever saw her do was de-husking dried melon seeds or on rare occasions, making laddoos of besan or roasted wheat flour.

I must have been four or five years old then.

I remember that she did not live with us. She visited us for a month or two every year. I went to the village sometimes with Ma and my younger sisters and sometimes alone, mostly in the summer vacation. Also we called the second one, not "dadi" but "bhabhiji" as did Ma and Pitaji. It was Pataji's tai, who was "dadi" to us and tai to Ma and Pitaji. The second one also never called Ma "bahu" or "bahurani", the way dadi did. Anyway, my image of bhabhiji was of one of her silently de-husking melon seeds or making laddoos, wherever she was, in the village or the city.

So when did she make the dolls? I remember the dolls well. In fact they were the only abiding link in our relationship. Whenever she came to visit us or I went to the village, she presented me with a doll on my arrival and one on my departure. Ma told me that she would make them herself with leftover rags. Of us three sisters, I was the only one to receive the dolls. My sisters felt jealous in the beginning, but gradually grew bored of the look-alike dolls as I did too. As I grew up, I began to feel embarrassed about them as well.

I guess Ma must have started telling me the second one's story at some point when I expressed my irritation with the ugly dolls and bhabhiji's morose presence, after her annual visit to us. As the story progressed in fits and starts, Ma said with deep contrition one day, "She turned this way only after her baby girl died. It didn't make any difference to anyone. No one tried to console her, not even I. We didn't even try to understand her sorrow, to say nothing of mourning with her. To tell you the truth, I was relieved when the baby died. Bauji was about to retire. We would have had to look after her along with you. Your father was never one to shy away from his duties. He had educated his younger brothers...but a sister as old as his own daughter... if he had to, he would have looked after her. But it was better that he didn't have to, wasn't it?"

Ma's story had awakened my interest in the second one. When I entered the world of teenage fantasies, at the age of fourteen, I said to dadi one day, "Ma says that bhabhiji used to sing ghazals. Why doesn't she sing now?" Ma was there at the time. Dadi looked at her with a hint of mischief as she said. "Lala said she'll learn the ways of a decent family, so she did."

Then she grew grave and added, "She gave up singing a long time ago. Soon after you were born." She would say no more. Ma's stories were also done. I was taking my first tentative steps upon the stage of life while bhabhiji had long vacated it.

I had discovered a new talent at that time. I had been drawing and painting ever since I was a child. Like in other schools, we had an art class, which I attended. My teachers praised my work and gave me good marks. By the time I was fifteen, I felt drawn towards portraiture. So I began taking lessons with a well-known artist, every evening after school.

I went to the village as usual that summer. The doll that bhabhiji gave me on my arrival somehow seemed to look like her. The budding artist in me became interested in bhabhiji's face. The next day when I saw her sitting and peeling melon seeds absent-mindedly, I decided to draw her. I took pencil and paper and planting myself in front of her, began to sketch. No words were exchanged.

After a while, I saw her hands slowly slacken and finally she stopped peeling the seeds. Her loose frame tightened and grew alert. Her neck and back drew up erect. A winsome smile played on her face, which she held at an arresting angle, as if she were a professional model or a vivacious teenager. I checked any expression of surprise and continued to draw, hardly daring to breathe. If only she would hold the pose!

After a while, she said softly, "I'm not pretty enough to be sketched. The first one was."

I felt relieved by the break in the silence. "How do you know?" I asked.

Her reply was startling, "From her pictures," she said.

What pictures? I had never seen any picture of a woman in the village house. Nor in the city house, not even of my revered nani. I remember, I had asked Ma if there was no picture of the first one for her to resort to trawling the second one's memories. Ma had laughed and said that it was not customary to take photographs in those days. People sometimes had paintings made, so she had asked tai if there was one of her first mother-in-law.

"Paintings are made of queens and empresses or of randis – prostitutes and dancing girls," was her tart rejoinder.

Later, seeing me paint portraits, Ma had let me into a secret. My nana used to draw too and he had made a portrait of nani but, following time-honoured tradition, had kept it locked in a cupboard. Ma had sneaked a look once.

Never mind nani, nana did not marry again. Ma had dreamed up all sorts of myths about her. But bhabhiji was talking about my real dadi now, not my nani. Was her picture locked up in a cupboard too? Where was it? When my sketch was complete, I leaned close to bhabhiji and whispered, "Do you have her picture?"

She snatched the drawing from my hand and glanced at it. An expression of deep astonishment spread over her face. "Is this me?" she asked. At that moment, she looked quite lovely despite her advanced age. Ma was right: she must have been rather attractive once. I gave myself a pat on the back. Good work, girl! Your portrait brought out the model's hidden charm.

"Please..." I stretched my hand to retrieve the sketch but she concealed it in the pallu of her sari. Her face grew tense. "If bauji sees it; that will be the end..." she muttered.

Of what, the sketch or her, I didn't quite understand.

"Don't tell anybody," she said.

"But..."

"Here, eat this," she thrust a handful of melon seeds at me and by the time I could gather them together properly, she had disappeared with the portrait. When I saw her later, she was back in her preoccupied posture, de-husking melon seeds, making laddoos, dead to the world about her.

I tried to sketch her again, once or twice. But she got up and retreated to her room, bolting the door, as soon as she saw me with paper and pencil. I could not understand why she had distanced herself from me. I told her, "I don't want the picture back. Please keep it..."

"Quiet!" she hissed, cutting me short; then she rose and left.

I thought, I won't get a doll when I leave. Good riddance. For many years, I'd been leaving her dolls with Bitto bua's children. She must have found out but she had never mentioned it to me.

When the time came for me to leave, Bhabhiji handed me a doll. One glimpse and my mouth fell open! None of her earlier dolls had displayed such refinement. The features, embroidered on the face with thread, were well chiselled, the figure of the doll exquisitely delicate and her clothes, well cut and dainty.

"This is like a painting!" I exclaimed, "You know drawing, do you?"

But Ma had said...

"Never mind me...you can draw...you are our... successor..." She muttered under her breath. I was so absorbed in the doll that I barely heard her words. I decided to take the doll with me. It was not a doll but a 'work of art'. These were the words most bandied round in my art class, 'work of art'!

I managed to show the doll to dadi despite the confusion attending my departure. She took one look and paled as if she had seen a ghost, "This...this..." she stammered as I went on brightly, "Wonderful isn't it? A living image of someone, created by an artist!" She was still muttering, "Yes, that is...this is..." when I made a quick exit. I needed to pack the doll in my suitcase. I could hardly miss the train because of dadi's inability to talk coherently.

I did not go to the village next summer. I had to sit for my board examination the following year, so had extra classes in school through summer. My art teacher had also promised to teach me some new techniques. I had to find time for that too. And time was in short supply. When you are nearly sixteen, there is so much to think about, friends and secrets and things to do, how could I leave the city to go to the village? It was the final year in school. There was much that I would have to leave behind when I moved to college. It was imperative to cherish the little time left.

We were in a celebratory mood, once the exams were over. All the cousins in the city decided to go to the village together for a short vacation. I was appointed *de facto* chief because I was most knowledgeable about the house in the village and had never let them forget it. But there came disquieting news from the village before I could enjoy my new headship. Bhabhiji had died. She had been suffering from an intermittent fever for a long time. She had asked for me often. I was not told about it because I was in the middle of my board exams.

All of us had to go to the village now anyway, so we did.

After the cremation, Bitto bua took me by my hand and led me to her room. She closed the door, then bolted it carefully. She opened the wooden cupboard and extracted a tin trunk from the clutter inside, concealed under a heap of old clothes. The trunk was dented and shabby with a rusty lock hanging precariously on a broken latch. She handed it to me with great ceremony. It flew open at the touch of a finger. My sketch of bhabhiji lay inside.

Why the elaborate secrecy? But it was not the time to crack jokes. I had not been allowed to look at it properly when I had drawn it. Not bad, I felt as I looked at it now. It could be framed and hung in our sitting room in the city. I picked it up for a closer look. I found another portrait staring at me from the trunk, most certainly not one of Bhabhiji. Still, the face looked familiar. The memory of her last doll flashed across my mind. I could see its face in the portrait. I put my sketch down and picked up that one carefully. Another picture lay underneath. The same face. I picked it up and found yet another. The room was caught in an illusionist's enchanted web. Magical! The pictures spread around me. I counted eight, apart from mine. They were far better than mine. In artistic expertise and the ability to capture the elusive beauty of the model. As far as my limited knowledge went, they were outstanding. So bhabhiji was a closet artist. I found it hard to believe. Hadn't Ma said that she had asked Ma to draw the flowers on her sari?

Quite bedazzled, I turned to bua and asked, "Did Bhabhiji make these?"

"No," she said, "the first one did."

"Whose face is this?"

"Her own."

Ah! So that's how bhabhiji knew what the first one had looked like. But how did she get the portraits? She had arrived at this house only after the first one had died. I guess dada must have given them to her? But bhabhiji had said...

However, bua was still speaking. "They are for you. She left them in my care, poor thing. You didn't come to see her in her last days. She talked of you constantly. Her own daughter had died so she poured all her love on you. But you didn't care..."

I had never heard Bitto bua talk like that before. Even If she had, would I have paid attention? I only knew her as bhabhiji's shadow and that too in Ma's narrative. One sang, the other accompanied her, or the two of them played chaupad. When one gave up, the other must have too. I remembered her as someone surrounded by children.

She continued, "When her sons were born, it was as if they were born to the first one. Nobody thought anything of her, ever since she came as a bride. She began to think of herself only after the third one came into her womb, the same time as you did in your mother's. She wanted that child so much, but it came to nothing. My children were born later but she never touched them. Not so much as a hug. It was only you she loved, so deeply."

I had never sensed the intensity of her love. But when did I ever take the trouble of looking at her? Bua had never said anything either. It was easy enough to make up stories after someone was gone. But what about the paintings?

"Who gave these to her – dada? Why were they stored in the trunk all this time? Why weren't they framed and hung somewhere? Was it not considered proper those days? Does my father know about them? What about tauji and dadi?" My questions came thick and fast.

"As if your dada would have preserved them! He would have burned them, had he found them! The way he burned the others. It was the second one, who was from the randiyon ka mohalla, not the first one. How could he let anything happen to sully her honour?"

"He would have burned her paintings! Why?"

"If a woman draws her own image looking at the mirror, how is she any different from a randi?" bua whispered with a furtive look at the bolted door. "Don't you stare at me," she added, "I'm only repeating what your dada said."

"Then how did these survive? And how did they come to bhabhiji..."

"After the first one died, your dada handed over all her things including the children to your tai-dadi, my mausi. Told her to use them herself or keep them for future daughters-in-law. The first daughter-in-law to arrive was the woman he married. Mausi gave her some of the ornaments and clothes and kept the rest for the others. But she dumped all the cast off clutter on the second one. The pictures were part of it."

"But didn't dadi open the trunk and look inside?"

"The pictures were not in the trunk, you silly girl! Bhabhiji found them inside the lining of an old mattress. She was opening it up to get it washed and re-filled when she found them. Nobody knows except me. She swore me to secrecy. Now you swear to me. You will not say a word to anyone!"

*Translated by Manisha Chaudhry*

# *Morass*

*Rajee Seth*

"Whatever I possess, however much it is, isn't it yours too?"

These were the very words that leapt into Aartee's mind but didn't find voice. Throwing such an emotional utterance on the dry rot of their life together seemed a farce to her, a mockery.

And there was no knowing how Amar would take it. When had he ever taken anything she said in the spirit it was said in? Worse, he'd sulk. Brood. Think his wife was killing him with honey in place of poison.

She got to her feet but didn't want to leave the room. Thoughts unspoken, incomplete, jabbed at her mind. Standing near the table, she set to throwing out the rubbish collected in the drawers. But the feel of solid matter in her hands did not translate into the sensation of touch. Her mind wouldn't be still. Was the disquiet dogging her heels still simmering somewhere inside it? Her mind should at least be clear before going to something else.

By now Amar had propped the newspaper up before his face. A screen. A covering. The covering she had to tear apart. And tell the person sulking behind it to breathe freer, easier. Tell him to snap out of it. That nothing had happened to drown him, to make him go under. It wasn't laid down anywhere that life had to function only according to his desires.

"I was saying something," she said, though she'd said nothing at all. She just wanted to draw his attention. "If only you'd got the bio-data ready, things would have gone smoother. It's already four or five days since my talk with Verma Sahib. We are the ones in need, all said and done."

Amar flung the paper down. "Nobody's that much in need. I don't want you dancing attendance on your boss under the pretext of our need. Everyone has needs, everyone has problems."

"You know Verma Sahib isn't that kind of man. I've told you so many, many times."

Verma Sahib is generous. He is protective towards his staff. But it was best not to launch into all that again. And as for holding a brief for Verma Sahib's benevolence, it would be courting disaster. His decency, his sincerity would be brushed aside as the partiality of a lecherous man.

Amar doesn't understand the constraints within which she has to labour. On one occasion, finding an opportunity, she'd asked Verma Sahib about a job for her husband. She's tried to keep him happy by taking on more than her share of work. An able assistant like her is not easy to find. She reduces his workload. She comes on time, draws up the drafts *he's* supposed to, chalks out his plans for him, and gives him good advice. Over and above her own position, she saddles herself with responsibilities that are not hers. But how long is she to toil like an ox? Kudos in the office don't come easy, not without problems elsewhere. The ceaseless tug of war between home and the outside world never allows her to derive any benefit from the money she earns – not that she's in love with the job.

When she decided to take up a job she'd reasoned that army people didn't always get peace postings* and seldom had their families with them. It was advisable, therefore, to keep herself involved with some work or the other. And then, in the army, who knew when … otherwise, office is blind routine, habit, and the drugged ease of basking in stable weather. What gold medals is she likely to receive from Verma Sahib? It's Verma today, it could be a Sharma or an Agarwal or a Niyogi tomorrow. Then a new routine would start, new plans drawn up. And work, loads and loads of work. After that, would come the precious nod of satisfaction from the boss, whoever it was. After that, the certificate of trust. And in all this, the salary remained the same.

Amar can understand what a delicate balance she has to maintain if he wants to. But he doesn't want to. He'd rather mope and wallow in the morass of his mind.

However, in the office these days, she really does hover around Verma Sahib like an invisible shadow. The office is her only space for hope and expectation. She's his P.A, true. But a great deal of motivation and initiative has come her

* Peace postings – as opposed to "non-family postings" in army parlance.

way these days. She deputises for him, free of the fear that he'd press her for any extra gratification. In a corrupt and calculating world, this piece of earth around her looks clean and pure. Within it, it is enough to be efficient, able and conscientious – the core rules, doubtless, of every office.

What is not in the core rules of any office, however, is the occasional – or these days, the more than occasional – cup of tea she has with him in the late afternoon. While pouring out his tea she is careful that no sugar strays into his cup. He is diabetic. Having this inside knowledge, she once ground a powder of methi seeds and jamun stones for him. Verma Sahib had taken it with much gratitude.

She asked him some five days later, carefully casual. "Did you have the powder, Sir?"

"Yes. I take it first thing in the morning in case I forget. We call it 'Aartee churan'."

"I could make some more, Sir."

"No, leave it to my wife now. She knows how to make it too. How much will you take on? Thank you so much."

The sky is caressing her head, Aartee feels. The sky never touches the head. But it's always there. Arched. Immanent.

During those dark days when Amar came home wounded from the army, she was PA to S.K. Mazumdar. He looked and behaved like a true heir of the Raj era. He projected a similar image of power – unsmiling face, hierarchical behaviour. The lines were firm and clear for S.K. You laughed or cried strictly with those of your rank, neither above nor below it.

To work with Verma Sahib after S.K. was to step into a realm abounding with human warmth and dignity.

Partly because of Verma Sahib's caring nature, and partly, no doubt, because it must have been buzzing all along in her sub-conscious, one day she opened up to him about Amar's accident. She told him about the shattering of his dreams, the dreams he had dreamt from childhood, of rising to the rank of a brigadier or general. And how quickly those dreams were shattered – within the twinkling of an eye! A full year hadn't passed since his promotion from second lieutenant to captain, when his leg was blown off while patrolling – from the knee down.

"Leg blown off?"

"He stepped on an enemy landmine. The lower part of his right leg vanished. The treatment went on for a year and more. The wounds healed, and an artificial limb was fitted. But it's not the wounds of the body that are the problem, sir. They heal. It's the wounds of the mind that continue to fester."

"He stays alone at home when you come to work?"

"No. His mother is there with him and my sister-in-law. My son too…"

For the first time she was opening up the doors and windows of her home. She didn't know that when you poured out your woes to someone, your voice came out so high, so frenzied. That in no time at all, your face convulsed with the agitation of the pain normally kept buried.

Verma Sahib was mature, experienced. He changed the drift of their conversation.

"But in such cases isn't a ground posting usually given? In other departments of the army?"

"They gave it all right, but he wouldn't take it. Teaching, staff management, administration…offers came from all sides. But he looked neither left nor right, simply asked for retirement. Harped day in and day out on how the lower departments in the army were unthinkable for a man of his qualifications. Wasn't he an alumnus of the National Defence Academy?"

Verma Sahib now looked up, surprised.

"You mean he's been idle since then?"

"No, not idle. But when your life begins to take a downturn you keep on sliding…" She told him how Amar had steeled himself to accept reality. How he had bridled the recalcitrant steed of his mind. She told him how, on a friend's advice, he'd put all his money into a cycle shop in the cycle bazaar off Panchkuian Road. Petrol was getting costlier day by day, he reasoned. The survivor would be the hardy bicycle, the only cheap and self-propelled mode of transport. He put his heart and soul into the work, though depression had him by the throat some days.

"I can well understand. It must have been tough going."

"No. It wasn't the work that was tough going. It was pitching camp in the middle of the bazaar, after all the style and polish of army life. The bazaar was a place of zero scruples, zero sense of right and wrong. Everything was weighed on the scales of crass profit. Paint and gloss were freely used to coat old goods. Sleight of hand ruled even for the sales of squeaky springs taken out of old mattresses. His spirits plummetted. Everything was in naked view here. Stripped of scruples."

"He left, then?"

"He didn't leave. Things left, just went. His capital went. A fire broke out one night and all went up in smoke. Short circuit? Arson? Who knows? The shops were stacked high with plastic and rubber anyway. What could have escaped? We got the news in the morning. By the time we got there all that met our eyes was a sodden and slimy morass. Maybe the fire brigade reached late. We knew nothing. What could we have done even if we had known?"

Verma Sahib lapsed into silence. What anguish lay behind such a glowing face, such ability amidst such trials! Such reliable efficiency... Why hadn't he given her a better Confidential Report last time?

His silence after her outburst unnerved Aartee. She regretted it. Did she *have* to open up her bundle of woes? You got respect as long as your situation has a tight lid in place. Remove it, and anyone could peer inside, see the mess, mock her.

"It's sad, very, very sad. I had no idea that... Let me see what I can do."

It was just a crumb of sympathy. But to Aartee it was like the security of a strong roof. She was overcome. However, it was forbidden to display emotion in these surroundings. "Excuse me, sir." She got to her feet. And wresting a kind of permission from him, she stumbled out of the room.

In the evening he called her in. He pressed her for Amar's bio-data. "If the details are there before me, I can put across his case well. I have spoken to Agarwal, by the way."

"Agarwal?" She gasped.

"Managing Director of Sarah Services. My bosom friend...says so at least..."

Back home she broke the news – to reap bitter taunts. Amar called it an underhand ploy by a superior officer. What did she know about such things? It was a man's world. Ask *him,* he knew…

After her bath, while getting dressed for office, she coaxed Amar gently. No matter what he said, she was determined not to let this chance slip by. What it took to create this opportunity, she alone knew. And she had no way of explaining or conveying her knowledge. And even if she tried to explain…

"I thought I could perhaps take the papers with me if they were ready. A day or two later you could go and meet him yourself."

"I've told you I'm in no hurry. I'm thinking of other things."

"Other things? What other things?"

"Other things. Now you get ready and go. Seen the time?"

He was right. She was late. She'd come to know in the evening, when she got back.

And what she came to know in the evening was shattering.

"With Bhaiji in Meerut, who is a builder," Amar said. "I'm going to work in partnership with him. He has years of experience. So what if we've been a bit distant from each other? You have to wipe out distances yourself. If one of your own kin happens to kill you, he'll at least take the trouble to throw your body in the shade."

"But...but," Aartee flared up. "Do you understand what this means? Understand anything? My job is here. Am I to leave it? Or go back and forth every day? Nothing's going to come of this! The family will be torn apart, not to mention other things. Is it a sensible idea?"

"You mean 'sensible' is only what you suggest?"

"I don't mean that. First let's just explore the paths that *are* opening up..."

"I've said what I had to! I've nothing more to say now!"

Afterwards, the same silence, the same face-off, the same pretence at being busy. Bridges lay broken. But why? If she could yield and make so much space for him, couldn't he offer her some space, respect too? At least as a return gesture?

When Amar went to sleep, something took hold of her. She turned the whole house inside out. And what she saw in his drawer struck her dumb. A fresh copy of his bio-data on top of his retirement papers! Three or four photocopies alongside, neat and clipped together!

Why hadn't he given them to her? Why this deception, this game of bluff? She felt hurt. But it was pointless feeling hurt. Had any value ever been attached to her feelings? This was the way things were, always would be. She should have been used to it by now.

The bio-data was carefully composed, very carefully composed. Amar had not had the slightest inhibition in writing about himself: not the least fear of overstatement, of laying it on thick. All his hobbies from childhood onwards, the contests won, the special skills acquired, the medals and trophies received at the Military Academy – it was all there, detailed accounts of each and every capability he possessed, everything he could accomplish, like a garment turned inside out. It wasn't easy, this art of not just projecting yourself in words, but showcasing your abilities.

Joy bubbled within Aartee now. The bio-data was impressive without question. She had no need to be beholden to anyone or feel apologetic. Of course, everything could go only so far, even with a bio-data like this one. Still…

Ever since the skirmish on the home front, Aartee has taken to keeping her lips sealed. The problems of home she leaves behind at its threshold, when she sets out for office. Ammaji manned the kitchen, looked after Anshu's needs too. But nothing more. She cannot sense that there is a third being in the house, also hungry for her mothering. She believed her son was a man now. Husband-less all these years, Ammaji had created a symbol of manhood in Amar for herself – the male who was to bear all on his own strong shoulders, and never be in need of any other shoulder to lean on.

Didn't Ammaji really see how heavy his load could be, after putting up with so many blows? When she tried now and then to awaken her to it, Ammaji snapped boastfully, "I do whatever he wants. He doesn't leave his room, do you know? Tells me to bring his food to him there. Thank god, Anshu is asleep by then. I carry his tray in. He eats sitting in his room, watching TV."

She could not tell Ammaji, what's so great about that, Amma? Fobbing him off with a nanny's services? Did you ever try to read his mind? What's so admirable about what you've been doing that you brag about it? At the very least, you could sit with him, or call him to you. It would lighten his oppressed heart. Help him pass the time.

But Amma had stopped being a figure of comfort for God knows how long now. She found fulfilment in wiping Anshu's mouth, cleaning his shit.

Every day, when she got back from office, she'd find Amma all set to push her feet into her slippers, not bothering to even change the sari, crumpled and stained by day long wear. From temple to home, from home to temple, the ledger of her life was being filled up. Suman, her own daughter, born of her own womb, was just as much out of her ken. Amma was afraid of tampering with her virgin state. Two years younger than Amar, the issue of her marriage had stayed put on the backburner for years now, for whatever reason or circumstance. Contributing handsomely as she did to the household, she could well afford to take her own time about getting married. And because of the bluntness of her tongue and her obstinate nature, nobody dared to bring it up. In any case, the one who's bringing in the cash will be absolved of a hundred sins.

The bio-data had come to her despite Amar. But she couldn't possibly act as his proxy. He had to meet Verma Sahib for a man-to-man talk. However, he remained indifferent. Luckily, the evening before, Verma Sahib had broached the subject himself. And Aartee got her chance. Before leaving for work in the morning she urged him: "Don't back out now. Be there before twelve. And come by my cabin first. This is a must."

She said this though she knew that she had to dispose off the Kishanchand Ramchand file today. It was imperative. God knows what was holding it up.

There are three people in the room now. One seated on the revolving chair. Amar facing him. Aartee on the chair alongside the revolving one.

Amar had received an effusive welcome from Verma Sahib. "Come in! You are most welcome. I've long wanted to meet you. Aartee never tires of talking about you." The papers of the bio-data rustled in Verma Sahib's hand.

"Your eligibility is beyond question. There oughtn't to be any problem. Corporates are always on the look out for an all-rounder like you. This is perfect!"

Amar's face reddened. "Hardly perfection…What I launched sank before my very eyes."

"It's a matter of chance. Happens sometimes. It's also chance, isn't it, that sometimes you press the right button as you are doing now, and set all the machines whirring?"

He glanced at Aartee at his side, at her face a-glow with the brightness of her lilac coloured sari. "Right, Aartee?" He smiled. She smiled too, as if in agreement.

Amar's ear lobes reddened. God knows what he read into this exchange. It seemed fraught with meaning to him, loaded. There had be something between them. Who did anything for nothing in return?

"I'd hate to see you going out of your way for my sake…"

"Now, why would I be doing that? Agarwal is a close friend of mine. Top man there. And you are no undeserving candidate either. Even without me you'd have made it. It's all chance, as I never tire of saying. Just give me a call in a few days, won't you? Things can slip out of one's mind, you know. They won't though, in this instance. Isn't she always around, never out of my sight?"

Something like the insistent beats of a street performer's drum thumped back and forth in Amar's chest.

Verma Sahib's hand reached for the bell. The peon came. An order was placed. In a short while the tea arrived. On the covered tray rested three rose-tinted bone china cups.

The tea tray infused the same energy into Aartee's hands as it did at home. She stirred the spoon briskly in the teapot, poured three cups, and held one out to Amar, still pouring in the milk. "Help yourself to the sugar."

"Verma Sahib first." Amar went formal.

"No, no sugar for him. It's plain tea for him always."

"And for you?"

"For her it's Diehard Dieter's Tea!" Verma Sahib laughed, enjoying his own joke, and gazed at her with teasing warmth.

They sipped their tea.

"If you folks would only come home some day, maybe I could take better care of you. Here it's just tea that I can offer. Aartee never tires of holding forth on the delicacies you fancy."

His familiarity jarred on Amar. So did the camaraderie of the sugarless tea. As if this place were like home – a shared space. And as if he had entered this place as a petitioner, not even a visitor. A petitioner asking for a job, after his own efforts had come to naught. And he hadn't even come on his own, he was brought here, by a woman. The best thing for him was to say…I don't want anything, thank you so much.

He suddenly felt that she was trying to read his face. Somewhat cowed down. An all-too-familiar current of futility coursed from her to him, him to her.

"So…", Verma Sahib held out his hand, stood up. "I'll do all I can. Take it from me." And he shook Amar's hand with warmth, firmness.

Amar held out his hand. "Thank you so much."

"May I…" Aartee now fixed her gaze on Verma Sahib.

"Sure, yes. See him off."

"No, you carry on. I'll be fine."

Aartee knew that stony voice only too well. She could have stayed back. The Kishanchand Ramchand file was yet to be disposed of. Before lunch was the time fixed for it. But she stepped out on numb feet. In the corridor she walked ahead. He followed. Aartee pressed the bell for the lift. It came. He left.

Back in the office she was tense, nagged by the remains of a tumult. The file was in her hands now. Verma lit a cigar, not seeming in any hurry.

"Good man. And how concerned you are for him."

Her heart leapt. But she squashed the impulse for a dialogue. She bent closer over the file, wearing a look of stern concentration on her face.

"Of course, it's but natural. I can understand."

Her silence continued.

He changed the subject. "The case must be dispatched for comments today. Delay will mean trouble. The hearing is next week."

She came back from wherever she had flown to. And she plunged into the file before her as if disposing of it was the only task in the world for her.

When she reached the office the next day, a message lay on her table. The clerk said that the boss had rung for her twice. She was late, she knew, but didn't want to be caught out. Amma was not well today. Suman had to give a maths test to her class, and couldn't stay back. Everything fell to Aartee's lot. She got late.

"Good news for your husband." Verma Sahib welcomed her, half rising from his chair as Aartee stepped in. "Congratulations. He should have been here in person to hear the good news."

She had never seen him this way before. His face wiped clean of the barest hint of authority. Even free of sympathy, which always pervaded this room like a soothing breeze.

She could only stammer, tossed between belief and disbelief. "Really? So soon? But how?"

"Do you know, Agarwal himself called. Normally they don't take outsiders. I knew it. But I knew too that he couldn't refuse me. And let me tell you, it's a good post. Branch manager. Within three years or four at the most he'll be..." Verma Sahib scanned her face. Perhaps he was searching for an outburst of elation.

But her face – it began to tremble before it could glow. Verma Sahib had never seen gratitude expressed in this way. Eyes turning moist even while making an effort to laugh with joy.

"I'm so thankful, sir...ever so thankful... I have no words to..."

"Relax..." Verma Sahib glanced away, controlling the waves of affection rising within him.

"Sir," she said hesitantly. "May I go and phone him? Right now?"

"Perhaps you should wait for the appointment letter?" Seeing her face fall, he said, "Go ahead. Tell him, there's no harm. If it helps. Between you two. Ring him from here..."

She sprang towards the phone like a bird released from a cage. Her hands trembled. "Hello! Yes, Aartee speaking. From the office. Please, Mrs Tyagi, can you call my husband from upstairs? It's something important. Yes, I'll hold the line. But I can't hold it too long, you know of course..."

As she waited, clutching the receiver, she explained, "Won't take a minute, sir. It's just the floor above. A short flight of steps..."

"Take it easy." He pulled the file closer deliberately.

"Listen, Aartee here. Listen...forget about leaving for Meerut today. You were going, weren't you? Don't go. Something's in the offing here. It's practically there. No, no... yes...I'm speaking from the office. No, from Verma Sahib's room. He sent for me just now. And told me! What? Never mind! What's a reservation slip? Tear it up! You haven't paid yet! Yes, I'm sure. I mean what I'm saying! Try to understand! What? Oh! All right, then. I'm putting the phone down. I said I'm putting the phone down. We'll talk at home..."

She put down the phone, but her face looked as if a voice had lashed it. A scream had rent it apart.

"Everything okay? Is he happy? I'm sure he is!"

"Yes sir. Yes sir. He's happy. Very happy." She stood up and began to walk towards the door. "Sorry, please call me when you need me."

"Certainly, certainly. You may go." A whole lifetime's wisdom and experience rang in his voice. The corners of his mouth sagged.

He called her later in the afternoon. She was alert and on her toes as always. But her eyes had a faraway look. As if engaged in battle on another front.

"I must thank you again, sir," she said, as she sat down.

"What do we have on our hands now? Which firm?' He spoke in very professional, clipped tones. It was the only rope he could throw to her to haul her out of herself.

Back home in the evening she found that he'd gone to Meerut by the afternoon bus. He'd left the keys with the neighbour. Suman had opened the door, when she got back from school.

"What time did he go?"

"Who knows?"

"Has Ramu brought the milk?"

"Don't know."

"And Amma?"

"Don't know."

She didn't ask about Anshu. And she stopped Suman from making tea for her. "Not for me."

"Had it in the office, I suppose!"

She turned to look at Suman. It felt as if she there was a

double meaning in her words. Everyone was being devious with her! She thought at first of reasoning with Suman who, like herself, dealt with the pressures of her job every day. Can't you see that I have to have a wash first, cook dinner, put Anshu to bed? I have to put the house in order, it's all upside down right now. Can I possibly enjoy a cup of tea and stretch my legs?

But she said nothing. Just asked for the strength to gather the four corners of her house, that were threatening to fly apart, into her hands. Asked it of herself. Only of herself.

*Translated by Raji Narasimhan*

# The Agony of an Artist

*Mamta Kalia*

We had known him ever since we moved into this colony. Almost four years. During this period, we spent a lot of time together, we lied, we loved, we clashed. The best part about him was that his temper cooled down along with his intoxication and his harangues did not outlive his hangovers.

In the beginning, he used to lie about his age. He would launch the topic, "When are you due for retirement?"

"Nine years from now." I would quickly do my cosmetic mathematics.

"And I thought you had twenty years. You don't look a day over forty."

"Thanks, but facts are facts." I cheered up at having managed to smuggle a few years into his imagination. After all, who cares for D-day? I could always say I opted for voluntary retirement.

Why would I tell him how much of aerobics, skincare lotions, hair dye and other precautions went into my youngness?

My husband was better insulated. He was two years older but he had neither greyed nor lost any teeth. His problem was the opposite. People asked him, "What brand of hair dye do you use? Your hair looks so glossy and youthful."

Anil simply smiled. He did not believe in explanations. He'd say, "Reality is so absurd. One has to labour hard to prove it. Why should I labour?"

But Mishraji did. He laboured not only for reality but realism. He worked towards creating a semblance of truth. He was unique in a number of ways and a cynic in others.

As a renowned director, he had staged some famous plays. With two pegs of Bagpiper inside him, he would become Dhritirashtra of *Andhayug* or Nana Phadnavis of *Ghasiram Kotwal*. He would vocalise the beats of a running chariot or the meows of a cat. He would recall his historic and histrionic highlights. The room became his playhouse and we, his audience. He would forget that theatre was now a dying art form. He'd say, "When I directed *Ghasiram Kotwal* people actually bought tickets for the show. Not a single free pass was issued. Just imagine, a crowd of one thousand strong watching my play in pin-drop silence."

"Potato chips did not have a roaring sale those days," I said.

"Shut up, you know nothing about theatre." He would drift off into memory lane. "For Gauri's role, I interviewed at least seventy aspirants."

Anil interrupted, "Don't exaggerate that much, Mishraji.

Where can you find seventy girl-aspirants in India? Parents usually dissuade girls from joining the performing arts. You might have screened seven or eight."

"No, at least seventeen girls had come for the role, I can testify," Mrs Mishra said.

From seventy we settled for seventeen. Mishra was wrapped in a fog of nostalgia. "There was a proposal to stage *Ghasiram* on Broadway but I insisted that we perform off-Broadway."

"Someone said there was a problem with your heroine."

"That was later. Initially we were good friends. But girls are so immature. We groom them into glamorous artists and polish their edges. They come to believe they are heroines in real life too."

"Kusum Verma's marriage was on the rocks. She acted as Lalita Gauri, didn't she?"

"I had nothing to do with that. Her husband Gaurav was my friend. He confided in me that she considered the whole house her stage and each family member a villain. If anyone said anything, she'd take centre stage in the room and start crying dramatically. Sometimes she made acerbic responses. If anyone reacted, she would say – it was a soliloquy, why did you overhear! When the two went out, she would be so heavily made up that it became awkward for Gaurav to accompany her."

Mrs Mishra observed an icy silence all this while. Obviously, the topic did not appeal to her. But for some time she endured it.

Old stories are like chronic aches, lingering, lovable, yet incurable. What was there to talk about in the present?

Newfangled theatre groups adapted European drama with much calculation and toured ten cities on a grant. They never cared to discover new Indian contemporary drama. They turned their backs on the vastness of life and the universe and restricted themselves to the reiteration of narrow issues.

We were aware of Mishraji's loneliness. His talent was being marginalised. Less deserving directors were taking over. His troupe had broken up. Some of the artistes were struggling to make it in Mumbai, in the world of television serials. Others registered themselves for jobs with the local employment exchange. The female artistes found the easy road to romance and marriage. Mishraji was left to sail through his evenings with the help of phone calls, booze and nostalgia.

It was December when we learnt that Manas Acharya, a comparative newcomer, was planning to set up a theatre institute in town. He had directed half a dozen plays but we had no idea whether he would be as accomplished in the field of academics.

Mishraji's mouth twitched when we told him about Manas Acharya.

Our glasses were brimming but he added an extra ice cube to each drink. They spilled over.

He laughed and bent his arms to form an imaginary bow and arrow. Then he aimed a shot at the table: "Shyon, shyon, shyon!"

Mrs Mishra put a finger on her lips.

He went and stood at the southern end of the living room, "So, Manas Acharya, you will teach acting. What do you know yourself? Do you know how to piddle? Well, go on piddling. Why don't you say you'll teach debauchery?"

Anil interrupted, "Manas was at the coffee house. He was talking of you in very respectful terms and wanted to invite you to inaugurate this institute. I gave him your phone number."

"You can't see why. He wants to shut me up, but I won't. I shall tell him to his face that he's a rogue."

"What will you gain by this?" Mrs Mishra got irritated.

"You are a stupid woman. A place for the pursuit of depravity is being set up in town and he proposes that I launch it. I, who have directed at least a dozen silver jubilee shows, including *Ghasiram Kotwal*. I, who directed a production of *Andha Yug* in this town, far superior to the one Alkazi put up at Ferozeshah Kotla. Oh, if only Bharti had seen the show! He would have penned another classic."

We slipped out quietly. This soliloquy would last long, we knew.

Even four years after his retirement Mishraji continued to go to the University to teach. His friends would ask, "You kept cursing the Vice-Chancellor, then why do you spend half your day here?"

"Who will complete the course for these students?" he said. "The fools have made me retire but there is no subsequent appointment. Already there are seven vacant posts in the Botany Department. Why should we blame students if they cannot recognise even four trees at the M. Sc. level? The existing staff is only interested in grabbing examinerships and viva tours. No wonder students have to go to coaching classes."

"You could take up coaching."

Mishraji would take offence. "Next you'll say – why don't you sell vegetables? "

The plants in his house proudly proclaimed that the place belonged not merely to a botanist but a boisterous genius. There were hundreds of potted plants on his terrace, a feast of flowers and ferns, crotons and cacti in all their splendour. He devoted all his spare hours to gardening. His garden welcomed us even when he was sullen.

Mishra did not believe in owning a house. He had lived in the University staff quarters and later moved to a rented house on an upper floor. Only on one occasion did his landlord make a comment on his terrace garden. He simply said, very politely, "You've put too many pots on the terrace. The water is seeping into the house. If you shift some plants to the ground floor, the place will look more attractive and the house will not get damaged."

Mishra flared up, "The seepage is because of the cheap and sub-standard material you have used in its construction."

The landlord was a bit of a coward. He apologised, "Please do not mind. It was just a suggestion. Do as you wish."

But Mishra began to hunt for a new house. Whenever he recalled the landlord's words, he'd get stressed and swallow a couple of extra pegs. His sons lived abroad and were well-off. He had visited both of them once but had come back, despite getting an immigrant visa. His sons were understanding and did not feel offended that their father preferred to live by himself.

Everyone has a routine and Mishraji too had set himself a routine that kept him busy through the day. In the morning, his garden, then his university classes, an afternoon siesta and four pegs in the evening, accompanied by discussion and nostalgia.

We were totally different. We belonged to the present. We loved our contemporary world in all its frivolity. I wasted endless hours watching telly trivia. If some channel flashed a 1965 film I changed it immediately. The stars of yesteryears seemed stale and silly with their dated outfits.

Sometimes we went to the culture centre to watch a play. On getting wind of it, Mishraji would accost us, "I believe you went to watch some trash."

Anil said, "Wasn't that bad a show. What with friends insisting..."

"Haven't you heard Jagjit Singh's ghazal, '*Dost ban ban ke miley mujhko mitane wale*,'" I argued. "It was the hundredth show of *Court Martial*."

Mishraji said, "Come over in the evening and we shall count the cracks in *Court Martial*. You Hindiwalas are so gullible. Some dimwit once wrote that *Court Martial* was a good play and for twenty years, you have stayed put on that. You don't believe in revaluation."

I persisted, "Revaluation does not mean you dump everything into the dustbin of history."

"Yes, you must. You must dump every tame effort and lame script into the dustbin of dissent and disapproval!" Mishraji shouted.

Very tactfully we diverted him from drama to the day's weather and his plants.

Sometimes we lost track of him. Days, weeks slipped by without any contact. Then early one morning he rang up.

When we launched into some polite small talk he boiled over, "Keep quiet! You did not care to phone me even once, though the telephone department gives you two free calls a day."

"We thought you were away."

"Don't tell lies! You thought nothing. I was just not in your thoughts."

Anil said, "You cannot imagine the challenges in my profession. The whole day passes in coming up with ways to push up the sales."

"Of late your paper has become a dead rat."

Now Anil lost his cool. "How can you say so?"

"You wrote nothing about the World Trade Centre's trauma. You are an insensitive journalist."

"Mishraji, my paper is purely local. Sometimes I venture into national coverage. But I will be neither here nor there if I try to become international."

"You lack global awareness. Your vision is narrow. Good-bye!" He hung up.

We were disturbed for a while, then became involved in our own routine. We could gauge his loneliness, so did not complain. We felt that memories and associations, tradition and experimentalism, activity and inertia were creating a commotion in his mind.

A new theatre journal, *Nikash* was being launched in Delhi and the editor called us to write an article on 'Drama at its Best in U.P.' with special emphasis on Allahabad.

Anil could not spare the time and I had always found reviewing theatre difficult. I said, "Why not get in touch with Mishraji? He is an authority on the subject."

The editor contacted him and Mishraji gladly agreed. He immersed himself in the project with great gusto. His consumption of alcohol went up. He kept calling friends to collect data.

One day he phoned us, "Come over this evening. I shall read out my article. A few more friends might come. If you give the green signal, the article will be finalised."

He was soaring high all evening. In between there was a power failure. Unlike other days, he did not become impatient but simply told his wife good humouredly, "Lady Macbeth, light some candles."

For a long time he held forth on the presentations of groups like the AAA, IPTA and Abhiruchi as if rehearsing the article. His very first peg went to his head. "I'll go to meet Nargis Gandhi one of these days," he said. "She'll fill up the gaps in my memory!"

We did not know Nargis Gandhi personally but were aware that she had acquired fame playing famous characters like Vasantsena and Shakuntala during the fifties.

Mrs Mishra butted in, "Suppose she fails to recognise you?"

Mishraji smiled. "I'll put on some makeup. Wait and see, once she hears my name she'll give me a big hug."

Anil said, "Don't worry about makeup. After all, time must have taken its toll on her as well."

"I never thought of that," Mishraji said with a glint in his eye. "Memories of your youth are like that, always as fresh as young green leaves."

"Leaves wither too," Mrs Mishra put in.

"Artistes do not age; the audience does. Great artistes are ageless. Oh! What grace she possessed. If she expressed Shakuntala's bashfulness, it would be like this – she would turn her face and hide her diamond nose stud." Mishraji imitated her. "It felt as if the sun had set on the stage. She was a Parsi, but memorised such lengthy dialogues so perfectly that the prompter was left stunned."

"You've found a good excuse to wallow in your memories", Mrs Mishra remarked.

Mishraji did not flare up. He had been transported to the year 1958.

"When did you see her last?" we asked.

He took a sip from his glass and smiled mysteriously:

*"She does not see me*

*I do not see her*

*But the knot*

*Belies the thread."*

Just then the phone gave out a shrill summons. He went to the gallery. After the exchange of greetings, some kind of argument seemed to follow, which was not audible to us. After a while we heard him banging down the phone. The he rushed to his writing table, grumbling all the while, and began to tear the pages of his article into shreds.

"What are you doing?" his wife interrupted him. "You've been at it all day."

Mishra flung the bits of paper into the air. He gulped down his drink and said, "That blockhead of an editor says that my article should not exceed five hundred words. How can you sum up the history of theatre in Allahabad in five hundred words? I have to write about at least fifty events. Which means only ten words on each. Am I a primary school student who has to count his words when he writes?"

"But why did you tear it up? You could have sent it elsewhere," I said.

"And be confronted with another ass? Who made an editor out of this fellow? He should have taken up a schoolmaster's job!"

The evening fell apart. We rose to leave. Mishraji accompanied us to the door to see us off, then suddenly changed his mind.

He slumped on the divan and said, "Just wait, some day I'll put up a new play, even if it's with a small troupe. Khuda hafiz."

*Translated by Mamta Kalia*

# Jagdamba Babu is Coming to the Village

*Chitra Mudgal*

Struggling to scrape off the dried up dough encrusted on the platter with a ladle, Sukhan Bhauji grumbles, "These modern day bahus! When they clear up the kitchen and put the dishes aside for washing, it doesn't strike them that they should be soaked!"

Her hands get chafed raw trying to scrub them clean. Because, if by chance, even a speck of grain is left sticking to a pot or pan, they'll be up in arms. They'll buzz like wasps, "Aiee, Sukhan Bhauji, it seems you've just rinsed out the dishes today. Can't you scrub them a bit? We're not asking you to do this for free – you get twenty rupees in cash, something to eat as well as gifts at every festival. Shall we start eating in leaf plates then, if you find it so hard to clean the dishes properly?" The one from Dinapur, the middle daughter-in-law, can riddle you through and through. It's not a tongue she possesses but a sharp edged chopper. Since she's dependent on them she has no choice but to sew her mouth shut and keep on working. But there was a time when she was so quick that the women barely had time to draw breath in between their jokes and she'd be through with her work. They say the Dinapur one belongs to a family of army men. That's why she's always ready to pick on others. Well, let her. As the old saying goes, 'You're so proud of your brass nose ring, if you had a gold one you'd take wing!'

"Hunh!..."

Sukhan Bhauji gathered up the clean dishes in a basket and was turning away when she heard Thakur Sumer Singh clear his throat at the threshold and stopped then and there. The daughters-in-law who were moving about, busy with their chores, sprang aside into the inner courtyard. This was his signal to those who observed purdah – that the master of the house was making an entrance. Tall, strongly built, Thakur Sumer Singh belongs to one of the foremost families of Bainswada. A proper char goinwala – the proud owner of four pairs of bullocks to plough his fields. Of course, the taluqdari is gone and with it all their former aristocratic grandeur. But an elephant remains imposing even when it is dead. Till last year he was elected as the village pradhan – the headman, regularly. This year Pandit Bhuvaneshwar Vajpayee trounced him. Of course, that hasn't made any difference to his bearing. His moustaches are as proudly pointed as ever. So what if the headship of the village has slipped from his grasp? He's still the secretary of the Youth

Congress for the backward classes. Hands folded behind his back, he crosses the vast courtyard on the right and goes and stands next to Didda, who's busy stuffing masala into red chillies for pickle. "Amma," he says, "Tell Sukhan Bhauji to meet me in my sitting room when she's through with her work. I have something important to speak to her about..."

"Is it about Lallona, Badkau? Is there a doctor coming from the city?" Didda tried to guess. Thakur Sumer Singh nodded in reply, "Yes, Amma," and was turning away when suddenly Didda remembered something. "Tomorrow's Puranmasi, Badkau... I want to pay my respects to Chandikan Swamiji. Will the cart be available early in the morning?"

"Yes, it will..."

He didn't give Didda a chance to ask any more questions nor display any curiosity about who would accompany her. He walked out of the house as quickly as he had come, his wooden sandals clattering as he crossed the threshold.

As she cleaned up the remnants of ash and food from the area near the drain, Sukhan Bhauji felt as if all her simmering thoughts about the Dinapur Bahu's ill humour had been tempered with a cool splash of water. She had overheard Didda and Sumer Singh's conversation. He was just like his father. Like a spring of fresh, soothing water hidden beneath hard earth. As long as the old master was alive he had taken good care of all his employees. It was matter of principle for him that no one who worked for him should remain hungry or unclothed. How could she forget that he had given her a pair of silver anklets when Lallona was born? Of the other three brothers, the two middle ones, Subhag

Singh and Sukhdev Singh, spent most of their time in the state capital. They say they run an ammunition factory there. In keeping with city ways, Subhag Singh has abandoned the Shergarh bahu and married someone else. Ever since she came to her in-laws' place after the gauna, even on the night of the kangan opening ceremony, she has not had the good fortune to enjoy the company of her husband. The city wife has three children. Sukhdev Singh comes and goes regularly. The youngest, the last product of the womb, Narendra Singh, is in the army. He's been receiving all kinds of proposals. But in spite of Didda's urging, Narendra refuses to get married.

Thakur Sumer Singh often advises Didda, "It's better not to force these modern boys…look what Subhag has done."

Didda's sorrow makes her cry out, "The Lambardar died waiting to see a bridegroom's crown on Narendra's head. It seems I'm not destined to see my youngest bahu's face either." Thakur Sumer Singh too, must be hurting inside to see that his words go unheeded. But like the sacred banyan tree, which affords shelter to all kinds of birds and bears the force of the wind and the sun and the rain unflinching, he continues to stand firm and straight…

After finishing her work, Sukhan Bhauji wiped her hands on her sari pallu and went and sat on the floor near Didda's bed as usual. She began to knead the fallen away flesh on Didda's calves with a gentle hand.

"How's your Lallona, Sukhan's wife?" Pushing the trough full of stuffed chillies aside, Didda grasped her hands and stopped her. The sudden sympathy made Sukhan Bhauji's sorrow spring up like a rash of hives.

"What can I say…he can't even walk properly… I've had crutches made from babool sticks…he uses them to go to school…yesterday he said," wiping her suddenly damp eyes with a corner of her pallu she made an attempt to control herself, "'My armpits hurt, Amma.' I checked and saw that he had been rubbed raw by the crutches."

Didda patted her shoulder consolingly. "Tch, tch, tch. When he's about to go to bed, heat some turmeric paste and smear it on his wounds. You must bear up. He may be lame, but at least you have a son to put Ganga water in your mouth when you die…" For a moment she was silent, then she said, in a choked up voice, "How does the Shergarh one keep heart…think of it, Sukhan's wife."

Sukhan Bhauji crossed the threshold and stood half hidden near the large sitting room, which was almost like the village assembly place. She could make out from the sounds of talk and laughter coming from inside that a large number of people were gathered there. How was she to inform the Thakur that she was waiting outside for him? Should she call out to one of the children? Otherwise she might just remain standing there. The day would pass and she wouldn't be able to meet him. Uncertain, she was about to turn away when someone saw her and Dukhi came out at once and asked her to stop, saying, "The master's coming, Sukhan Bhauji."

Hearing the sound of the wooden sandals approaching, Sukhan Bhauji pulled her sari pallu down, right up to her nose. Her heart beat faster, like a madly pounding grinding stone. Even though, after having overheard his brief conversation with Didda she knew why he wanted to have a word with her, it was the first time she had spoken to Thakur Sumer Singh alone. It was natural that she be terrified.

"The former health minister, Jagdamba Babu is coming to the village. He wants to find out...listen to problems of the people..." Thakur Sumer Singh started off without bothering to fill her in on the background. "He has organised a 'Viklang Uddhar Samiti'. This body is trying to help the disabled to be self-reliant. His aim is to make the crippled and lame live as equals in society. I've informed him about all the disabled people in this area. The specialists from the district hospital will come and examine everyone. They will be helped according to their needs." To make things clearer he continued in simpler language. "If artificial limbs can be fitted on some they will be...the others will get carts which they can move with their hands. From our village, I've given in your son's name. The doctor's coming tomorrow. Bring Lallona to the sitting room around ten in the morning. After a few days there'll be a gathering at the wrestling grounds and Jagdamba Babu will distribute these gifts to the disabled."

Unable to believe that he was actually saying all this, Sukhan Bhauji was overwhelmed. She bent to touch his feet and express her gratitude. Barely had she raised her head, when he returned to the sitting room without another word. Overjoyed, Sukhan Bhauji felt as though it was not Thakur Sumer Singh who had been standing near her a few moments ago but some godman with supernatural powers.

When she stood up she felt as if her work-weary frame was as light and carefree as a flower tossing on its stem in the breeze. The fifteen-year-old yearning to see Lallona moving about easily has not given her a moment's peace. Neither to enjoy a morsel of food nor to laugh and talk comfortably…

What hasn't she tried? Vaidyas and hakims, all kinds of magic potions and rituals – but neither herbal medicines, nor prayers, nor the special rites worked. Lallona's lifeless legs remained as they were.

As soon as she entered her locality and saw the children setting off in a group with their slates and school bags, an unwonted gleam lit up her tired eyes. Lallona also insisted on going to the madarsa with Bakrihain Kaki's Bhaggoo. Limping along on his crutches. Bhaggoo had reassured her, "Don't worry, Nania…I'm there with him." He carried Lallona's slate for him. Earlier she used to go every day and leave him at school. But it was hard. If she were even a minute late the daughters-in-law's tongues would start lashing out like oil soaked whips.

How sweet the children look! All of them have a large wooden slate tucked under an arm. In the other they carry inkpots. Is that her Lallona – the tallest and strongest looking one in the bunch, on the right side of the lane? The fine dust, like powdered cotton, coats his bare feet… only the striped drawers swinging on his thighs look like an ugly patch on his beautiful body. She won't send him to school like that any longer. All the boys his age wear pyjamas. She has scraped together a few paisas – painfully saved – and buried them in a pot in the kitchen. With the thought that they would come in handy when times were hard. But what good was money if her child went about shabbily dressed? If he didn't discover the good things in life now, he would never learn to appreciate them and any small luxury set before him would be like offering sweets to someone who's fasting.

In spite of the crowd of children surrounding him, her restless heart urges her to dash forward like a runaway cow and press Lallona to her heart and tell him she would have a kurta and pyjama stitched for him right away. She'll get a pair of chappals for his feet too. Won't the Dhanuhi Kheda market be held this Thursday itself?

"Chachiya, pranam! Chachiya, chachiya, Lallona's class has been punished by the head master. They've been made to stand in the sun…he won't let them go for an hour at least…some mischievous fellow broke the water pot."

Hearing the epithet 'Chachiya' from Lallona roused her from her deep slumber. It wasn't Lallona but Subhangi Didiya's son. What dreams had she been seeing!

Hearing about the punishment, her leaping heart sank low. He had eaten only a left over roti with some buknu – a digestive spice powder. He must be dying of hunger. And, as if that wasn't enough, there was the agony of the wounds in his armpits. For a long time she had been thinking of padding his crutches with pieces of old dhoti so that they wouldn't dig into his armpits. But all the cast off dhotis that came her way from Thakur Sumer Singh's household went to cover her shame. What a lot of effort is needed to heal those chafed armpits!

Opening the lock with the key tied to her pallu, entering her hut, Sukhan Bhauji's heart kept veering between hope and hopelessness. Would the little flame of expectation that Thakur Sumer Singh had lit actually keep burning? It is possible that a miracle might take place. What vaidyas, hakims and tantriks cannot accomplish, city doctors with their stethoscopes achieve these days.

One hears all kinds of things. Kalicharan who drives the headman Pandit Buvaneshwar Babu's jeep was telling her about his own experience. "You see this left leg of mine, Sukhan Bhauji. It's not real – only the flesh on top is. I crashed into a truck one day and shattered it. I had given up all hope of ever being able to earn my living again. But Bhauji, I have to give credit to these Loknayak Hospital people. Instead of a bone they've inserted a steel rod so cleanly that I've been saved from being dependent on others.

Kalicharan is not one to make up stories. He had exposed his leg to show a long scar, the sight of which had caused a sympathetic gasp to burst out of her mouth. If Kalicharan could be set right – why not Lallona?

After telling a curious Lallona to lie flat on the table the doctor bent over his grimy frame with his stethoscope. He lifted up those wasted legs a bit, tried to bend them, pinched and pulled and pressed his withered toes, shrivelled like dried up bean pods. In between he would try to gauge Lallona's reaction and kept asking whether any of those actions – pulling, pressing pinching, lifting and suddenly dropping his legs made him experience any kind of sensation.

"Were his legs lifeless from birth?"

Flustered by all these proceedings, Sukhan Bhauji was unable to open her mouth in reply. She was a woman who observed purdah, how could she talk to a strange man? And even if she ever did, it was in the company of her peers. Here Thakur Sumer Singh was present along with the Lambardar Putan Singh of Manjkuria Tola, Pandit Matadin Tewari, Rajau Kaka – all her elders and betters. How could she dare to open her mouth in front of them? If, ever, by chance she happened to come across any of them on the road or in a doorway, she would quickly turn aside and stand silent and still till they had passed.

The doctor understood her hesitation. Gently he said, "If you feel shy I cannot come to any conclusion…the treatment will be delayed…no one else can answer my questions properly."

Suddenly Rajau Kaka turned his attention on her. Abandoning the conversation, he said gruffly, "Why are you troubling the doctor babu? Tell him whatever he asks."

The doctor repeated his question, "Were his legs useless since birth?"

Sukhan Bhauji was able to muster the courage to shake her head.

"How can you say his legs were all right?" the doctor asked.

"He used to toddle around the courtyard." Sukhan Bhauji's throat constricted as she said that. It was hard to keep a hold on her emotions. The old memory of Lallona's babyhood, staggering about delightfully with a black tika on his forehead, surged up before her eyes.

"So, when did his legs stop working?"

Trying to keep a tight grasp on her tears, she said in a choked voice that he had suddenly fallen over on his belly one day and remained like that. She had massaged his legs with mustard oil and God knows what other oils but life had not returned to those useless legs.

"It's a case of polio." The doctor gave his diagnosis to Thakur Sumer Singh who had come to stand next to him. "It's too late for any remedy. Timely treatment could have helped...if his legs were broken or amputated, some treatment would have been possible. Artificial limbs could have been fitted. The only thing for him now is to go on crutches or a wheeled cart...I'll tell Jagdamba Babu."

"I'll be meeting Jagdamba Babu in the morning at the District Office. Day after tomorrow the party secretary is coming from Delhi. We have to discuss matters concerning the party organisation. I'll speak to him. How many villages have been covered?

"From your neighbouring village Dhanuhi Khera to Bara...there are not too many cases of disabled people... mostly children. This is the problem in the villages. Many children are crippled by polio."

The Thakur looked serious. "You're right...people are illiterate and superstitious here. Even when the vaccination is available they will not get it done. Shall we leave for Bharatipur after some tea and snacks?"

"Tea and snacks at Vasudev Babu's. It would be good if we could cover the next three villages in this block by the evening."

Leaving Thakur Sumer Singh sitting there the doctor's eyes fell on Lallona's dark frame swinging along on his crutches. He turned to Sukhan Bhauji with a sympathetic glance. "Stop worrying. You'll soon find your son roaming about with other boys his age. His legs cannot be healed.

But there's no need to lose hope. I'll ask Jagdamba Babu. They can give him an invalid chair..." He stepped forward to pat an apprehensive Lallona on the shoulder. "Your arms will take the place of your legs, my boy...but just take care of your health."

Doctor Babu's reassuring words made Sukhan Bahuji's heart overflow with hope. Her innocently trusting heart imbued the unseen Jagdamba Babu with the image of a miracle-working god and her eyes rained tears as if in homage to this deity. The doctor spoke the truth when he said that Lallona should take care of his health. Why else has she kept a goat? But sometimes greed gets the better of her. The lure of a few rupees compels her to cook the milk into khoya. May she be cursed, may worms eat her if if she even dreams of doing that now...

As she drew closer to home she discovered that news of her Lallona's legs being treated by the doctor had spread through the village like wildfire, generating almost as much excitement as the news of a visit by Salone Bhai's nautanki. When people accosted her saying, "After fourteen years even the most unfortunate of creatures finds its luck turning... Truly Bhole baba has had mercy on a mother's woes," she wiped her eyes and lavished praise not only on Thakur Sumer Singh but also Jagdamba babu. Everyone agreed with her...hadn't Gandhi Baba helped the suffering people and brought swarajya? And after him it was Vinoba Baba who donned a loincloth and went from village to village helping the hopeless. Jagdamba Babu seems the same godly type of being. Otherwise who cares to apply balm on the sufferings of the poor?

"It's all due to Thakur Sumer Singh's greatness. As for the pradhan, Bhuvaneshwar babu, he's too busy enjoying his headship...he was only bothered about the poor as long as he wanted votes...now if anything worthwhile is taking place in the village it's all thanks to Thakur Sumer Singh."

The woman member of the State Congress Committee was able to persuade Sukhan Bhauji to sit on a chair only with great difficulty. That too in the very last row. About fifteen or twenty feet away from the high, machan-like stage, bedecked festively with strings of marigolds. Sukhan Bhauji was able to muster the courage only after seeing all the women who sat on either side of her, bare-headed with badges pinned importantly to their shoulders. They had come from Nakhlau (Lucknow). She could not remember if she had ever occupied a seat higher than a string cot or a stool. That too among people of her own class and caste. In Brahmin or Thakur households she found the bare ground the most suitable seat available to her.

Casting an eye full of silent joy from behind her ghunghat, she glanced up at the chairs arranged on the right side of the stage. All the disabled sat there. She thought of Jagdamba Babu. Everyone says he is a true servant of the people. The protector of the poor. He was the health minister in Guptaji's ministry. Guptaji, who understood their sufferings. In the last election, somehow the stars betrayed him. He lost this stronghold that had been his for years on end. A person like Gayadin of the Janata Party overthrew him by just 700 votes. The ballot boxes had been changed by force. Otherwise how could a crook like him win over an honest man like Jagdamba Babu? What made things worse was that both the Collector and S.P. turned out to be from his caste. Else who would vote for a characterless man like Gayadin? Wasn't he caught red-handed having a good time with Shivlal's daughter, Sukhni, in Bhusaur. Sukhni's brother had chased them up to the big canal with a fodder-cutting chopper. Later, he had had him sent to jail on a trumped up charge…that he had been trying to break into Thakur Shivbali Singh of Bharatipur's house. If such a person could win against Jagdamba Babu it could only be by foul means. He may have made it to the Vidhan Sabha but he hasn't shown his face in the constituency three times in three years. He's given out permits and contracts to all his close friends and relatives, opened liquor shops and had ordinary gravel spread on some roads in the name of public service. He had said he would have a big hospital built in Dhanuhi Kheda and put in a special thirty-bed maternity ward so that both mother and child would receive proper care but there's no sign of even the foundation stone being laid. So what if his party isn't in power? Why did he make those promises? They say that Jagdamba Babu who's coming to help the poor is not spending from the government funds. He is going to open up his own purse strings to buy sewing machines, crutches and wheelchairs to give to the lame and crippled. He has truly devoted himself to the service of the poor…

How wonderful everything looks! It's just like at the Mahavirs' fair. The two-mile long wrestling ground is all decked out with flags and buntings. Gandhi Baba's "Raghupati Raghav Raja Ram…" is booming over the loudspeaker. In between they play the last speech Indira

Gandhi gave before her death. The public has travelled for miles on foot, bullock carts, jeeps and trucks. They're saying that newspaper people have come from distant places to cover the event and take photographs, and news about everyone and their photos will be printed in the newspapers.

Sukhan Bhauji longs to ask of the ribbon-badged Behanjis, so busy with the arrangements, to show her the invalid chair from close. So she can touch it and imagine Lallona sitting on it and moving about on it. She won't have to apply turmeric on his festering armpits any more. They soak up so much that often there's not even a pinch left over to put in the dal.

Her eyes roam all over and finally rest on Lallona seated next to the stage. He's wearing a new markeen shirt and khaki shorts, looking like a prince out of a fairy tale. She had borrowed a handful of mustard seeds from Bakrihain kaki. Ground them as fine as she could and rubbed off all the dirt from his body with it. After he had bathed and dressed she had suddenly been painfully reminded of his father. He had left them and departed one day, carrying his longing to see Lallona get up and walk on his legs with him.

The sun has climbed over their heads and is beginning to scorch now. They're saying that Jagdamba Babu will reach the wrestling ground by eleven o'clock. After the programme is over he'll meet the headman of the village, Bhuvaneshwar Babu. He'll listen to the people's grievances in private as well. And carry them straight to the government. He'll try his best to see that some action is taken as soon as possible. After that the whole entourage will have lunch in the madarasa.

Suddenly, clouds of dust raised their heads along the tarred road. The organisers sat up alert. Thakur Sumer Singh got onto the stage and announced in a loud, stirring voice that their patience had finally been rewarded. In just a few moments the well-known social worker and founder of the 'Viklang Uddhaar Sabha' would grace the meeting. "Kindly remain seated in your places as you welcome him. Show your enthusiasm, but remember your manners," he added.

Some men armed with big sticks had been placed as guards all around the meeting place just in case people from the opposite party, particularly the pradhan's followers, created a disturbance.

The moment Jagdamba Babu's jeep halted, the gathered multitude greeted him joyfully. Thakur Sumer Singh sprang forward to escort him to the stage. A procession of government functionaries, from the Block Development Officers upwards, followed. Though he was no longer a minister, Jagdamba Babu still commanded a certain amount of clout as one of the organisers of the ruling party. Everyone knew about his connections that reached right to the top.

The celebratory mood got to Sukhan Bhauji. First of all, she had been granted the privilege of being seated among the higher ups because of her disabled son – an honour even mothers of sons with well-paid jobs could not dream of. And secondly, her disabled son would soon be able to stand up on his own feet now. Her joy seemed to buoy her up, filled each fibre of her being. Her eyes would wander from the garland laden Jagdamba Babu on the stage to Lallona's astonished face.

"Bhaiyon! Now Jagdamba Babu will distribute gifts to the physically disabled which will make them self-reliant…" The audience clapped loudly when Thakur Sumer Singh made this announcement.

Jagdamba Babu got down from the stage and moved to the spot where the gifts were on display. The tired, dispirited faces of the disabled lit up the way the hundreds of earthen lamps floating on the Ganga in the evening brighten up its waves. Names began to be called out…

"Sankatha Prasad of Sagwar, who does not have the use of his right hand…" Jagdamba Babu gave him a sewing machine he could operate with his feet. Sankata Prasad works in Jumman Miya's tailoring shop. He can set up his own now. Jumman Miya will help him out by cutting the garments for him… Jagdamba Babu stands on one side of the machine. Sankata Prasad on the other… Sukhan Bhauji is gripped by a sudden apprehension. The names are being called out, turn by turn. Why hasn't Lallona been called till now? Suppose all the gifts get distributed and nothing is left for him? Then as more names were announced, she exclaimed, "Mori dayya, that's my Lallona's name!" Suddenly as bashful as a young maiden, Sukhan Bhauji bites her lip. She's so used to calling him Lallona that it didn't register… Bishnu Kumar Bari is none other than her own Lallona.

From where has the child acquired so much strength? Leaning on his crutches he's stumping his way towards Jagdamba Babu who is standing near a bicycle-like vehicle with one handle. One of the badge sporting organisers introduces Lallona to him. Lallona folds his palms and says, "Namaste," to Jagdamba Babu. Tch, tch! Shouldn't he touch his feet instead of saying namaste like a babu? Sukhan Bhauji's head buzzes with shame. But the very next minute she realises her mistake. How could Lallona bend over, leaning on his crutches?

A beaming Jagdamba Babu, scissors in hand, is explaining something about the vehicle to Lallona. Thakur Sumer Singh moves forward and asks him to cut the pink ribbon on it. The moment it's snipped through the sound of measured clapping electrifies the air. One of the organisers is showing Lallona how to sit in the vehicle and drive it with the handle. Lallona's startled eyes gleam with a sudden confidence. He has seen numerous bicycles racing through the village, the pedals pumping, propelled by moving feet. He feels as though his hands have turned into those feet, the handle into a pedal and his feet are moving swiftly on the pedals...

Lallona's vehicle moves bumpily but speedily on the uneven ground... The resounding cries of the fully charged crowd fill the skies with their clamour.

As soon as Lallona returns to his place after describing a large circle, Jagdamba Babu pats his back and congratulates him. Photographers surround both of them. It's an amazing sight for the simple village folk. A good-hearted woman organiser remembers Sukhan Bhauji and makes her get up, forces her way through the crowd and tells the photographer that this is Bishnu Bari's mother. They want to take her photograph with Lallona and the vehicle. But in spite of their continuous coaxing, Sukhan Bhauji will not lift her ghunghat even an inch. It's a good thing she didn't, otherwise what would people have said? Her streaming eyes would have been exposed and they would have said, "What an inauspicious woman! Shedding tears at such a joyful moment..."

After putting away the left-over food in the hanging basket overhead for fear of the cat, Sukhan Bhauji became anxious about giving Lallona his milk. The moment he falls on his bed he begins snoring, the Kumbhkarna. She'll wash the dishes later. Just mother and son...how many utensils do two people use in any case? But she won't leave them for the morning. It's ekadashi tomorrow. She has gathered cow dung from the road to plaster the house. Unless she gets up while it's still dark she will not be able to complete the job till the sun comes out. If she's late for work, can those daughters-in-law even dream of losing such an opportunity to scold her?

At the right corner of the courtyard – where she's planted mint and where the gourd creeper clambers up the shapeless mud wall, Lallona's cart stands. She does not dare leave it outside the door. They had to break the threshold, level it down so that it could be brought inside. He whizzes into the courtyard, circles round and round, teasing her. Harassed, she scolds him, "What do you think you're doing...trampling all the mint? If you show off like that I'll flay your hide, just you wait and see." He will carry on, teasing her to the point till he realises that she really will translate her threat into action.

She poured out milk into a glass and added a thick skin of cream on top. Holding the warm glass with her sari pallu, Sukhan Bhauji was advancing towards Lallona's cot when she heard someone rattle the door chain. Is this her imagination? No...it's real. The door chain is rattling. There is someone at the door! Putting the glass down by the cot, she picks up the oil lamp from the alcove and moves towards the door. It must be Bakrihain Kaki. Her daughter-in-law is ready to give birth. It's possible that her pains have begun and she's come to call her to help.

"Is it you, Kakia...?" Sukhan Bhauji called out, full of assurance.

"It's me, Thakur Sumer Singh," a deep voice boomed in reply. Sukhan Bhauji recognised it at once. The master, and at this hour? Could something terrible have happened? Could it be Didda...? But even then he wouldn't have come on his own to call her? Dukhi, Bharose, Dulare anyone of them could be sent running. She lifted the lamp high and raised herself on her toes to open the door, drew her ghunghat over her head, standing in the shelter of the door. It was hard to decide how to welcome Thakur Sumer Singh in. It was the first time he had appeared at her door. Where could she ask him to sit? How could she ask him why he'd come? He solved the problem himself.

"I have something important to say to you."

The blood coursed swiftly through Sukhan Bhauji's veins.

"Actually tomorrow there's another gathering of the 'Viklang Uddhaar Samiti' at Vighapur. Jagdamba Babu is going to present gifts to the handicapped again. It is possible that the central minister for energy might grace the occasion. The programme has been announced but the vehicles haven't arrived. The TV and newspapermen, as well as many highly placed people have been invited.

Thousands of people from nearby areas are expected to gather there. The elections are close. It is impossible to cancel the programme…the vehicle that was given to Lallona is wanted back!"

Saying this, his eyes roamed searchingly in the wavering light shed by the oil lamp and seeing the cart standing in a corner of the courtyard, he said in an unexpectedly gentle voice. "We'll get a strong pair of crutches made for Lallona…our aim is that he should be able to move about comfortably."

It was as though Sukhan Bhauji had been struck by lightning. She wanted to throw down the lamp clutched in her tightened fingers and fall at the master's feet like a freshly cut tree. "Master…don't snatch away my child's life… Lallona prances about like a leaping deer after getting the cart…he's the only hope of a helpless widow…if you take the cart away how will he live…"

But the sheer terror of Thakur Sumer Singh's presence silenced the wail that reared up inside her.

Thakur Sumer Singh left her standing there petrified. He called out to the three men who were waiting outside for a signal from him. Without bothering about Sukhan Bhauji's lack of response, he ordered, "Pick up the cart carefully and put it in the van. Don't take the van through the lane but the road that runs through the uncultivated land."

Then he turned to Sukhan Bhauji who stood there trembling, trying to contain the cry that buffeted back and forth between her belly and her throat, "If anyone asks… say it was stolen."

On shaky legs, Sukhan Bhauji closed the door and entered the little room. She lifted up the oil lamp she was clutching to light up the wall on which a scrap of newspaper was pasted. It had a picture showing Lallona seated on the cart and a beaming Jagdamba Babu clapping his hands...

*Translated by Deepa Agarwal*

# The Dispossessed

*Chandrakanta*

No one had ever imagined that this could happen! Despite knowing that anything could happen these days – no one had believed it really could.

Hiding their shame under gunny bags, the families stuffed like cattle inside the shelter – a half-finished sarai with gaping door frames – had not imagined it. They who had traversed all the conceivable boundaries of humiliation and dread, obstinately holding on to a fistful of breath, while constantly living with the terror that anything could happen at any moment.

And as for Laspandit: how can a man be expected to think after all the nuts and bolts in his mind have slipped from their moorings? Say land, he'll think it's the sky! Perhaps people are right when they say so – but did Laspandit lose his mind without reason?

Were those mere commonplace abuses? They did not

give him time to even lift his forehead – bent low in prayer at the threshold of the temple. When the two young boys – the lower part of their faces covered with black scarves – dragged Laspandit and flung him on the ground, ignoring his mud-caked wounds, he tried to recognize those half-concealed faces even while reaching out to save his grimy, sodden turban.

"*Arre*...*re*...yo-ou?" Shiva, Shiva! Laspandit's tongue twisted when recognition seared through. " Subahaan ju's son ...what are you doing? Why...why?"

Subahaan ju is after all Laspandit's friend. The difference in faith and religion has never been a hurdle in their closeness. His own son...? And this Shabbo...? He is Phaata the dairymaid's son, isn't he? No, no, how can this be possible?

That very day, for the first time, Laspandit's treasure house of knowledge began to fall apart seeking an answer to the question, 'how did all this happen?' Later, the calamity that struck Jaya demolished whatever little had survived.

But who is this man alternately known as Laspandit, Lasboya, Laskaakor, Lasgor? It's about time you get to know him. Actually, it is absolutely essential. Why? You will soon know the reason.

Laspandit, son of Madhava Pandit, home and village – Matan, the place where the famous Martand sun temple stands, which Lalitaditya Muktapeed began to construct in 699 A.D. It was completed much later. About forty miles from Srinagar in the Kashmir valley – once an incomparable paradise – proudly stand the ruins of the temples of Martand – witnesses of a long past glory. A mere glimpse of these elegant architectural marvels brings forth the spontaneous response, "Ah! Such grandeur – even in ruins!"

So, Matan village is right there, with its spring of clear, unpolluted water – just like aabe hayaat, the spring of immortality! Abul-Fazl has referred to it in *Ain-i-Akbari*. The Brahmins of Matan believe that the souls of ancestors achieve fulfilment through shraddha – offerings and worship for the dead – performed at this sacred spot. Here Laspandit performs various kinds of rituals. From shraddha to major and minor ones like havans or fire sacrifices, mundan – the tonsure ceremony or the sacred thread ceremony, *janeu*, marriages, and prayers for thanksgiving or seeking boons, he conducts all these ceremonies correctly and with reverence. Visitors who came to Matan do not fail to search for him. His profession may be ancestral, but he has earned the prerogative of being called 'pandit' by studying the Vedas and Shastras deeply. He would have otherwise been known as 'Lasgor' and might have stood waiting in a queue like ordinary priests. Do you think rich and knowledgeable clients would have pursued him then?

A fistful of bones comes together to constitute lean and skinny Laspandit, who bends his head low to greet respectable people. He may be a contented soul but is hardly an ascetic... Rather, he is the head of a fairly large household. His eldest son Gasha having completed his post-graduation, teaches science in a local school and in his heart despises his father's occupation as the 'profession of paupers'. He has an accomplished, pretty daughter, Jaya, whom the village people refer to as a lotus blooming in mire, and at whose birth Laspandit had felt that the goddess Ragya herself had appeared in his home. Mother Shobhawati had become a little anxious that later she would have to protect this fragrant budding rose from the black bees hovering around. And Shobhawati's last born Babli, who is still unformed – like an unbaked clay pot. It is difficult to say anything much about her yet.

Laspandit's wife Shobhawati is of course a complete homemaker, like any other housewife. From dawn to dusk she keeps company with the sieve and the winnowing basket, the broom and other household tools, besides attending to the cattle, along with other odd jobs in the village and at home. She hurries here and there scolding the children under the pretext of teaching them, and is truly the Annapoorna – the goddess of food and prosperity – of the family. With what relish she cooks green wostahaakh, turnips and lotus stems, grown in her kitchen garden and tries to read her children's faces to guess how it tasted. She also fulfils her responsibility as a wife, by taking her husband to task for his occasional slips.

Ah...the bitter-sweet flavour of family life with its small squabbles! On the whole, Laspandit's life was progressing rather well.

People did not address him as 'Laspandit' without reason. He was not one to rush through any holy ritual saying 'Om-yom-yom' to save time, and never misread or mispronounced the shlokas or performed any puja casually – without the appropriate reverence or devotion. Instead, he scrupulously observed all the tenets of dharma and was careful to follow the established form as laid down in the scriptures while performing ceremonies. He would only accept any offering when he had done this. Apart from that – if Guddi's horoscope had to be prepared, the position of Radheynath's stars to be interpreted, mantras to be chanted to remedy saadhesaati – the inauspicious seven and half year period and other such ill-omened phases, Laspandit was the one everyone looked for.

The sarvakamnasiddha mantra that fulfilled all desires, bhayanashak mantra that put an end to one's fears... was there any mantra that Laspandit did not know? As for the mantra against adversity, it was constantly on the tip of his tongue. Moreover, so melodious was his voice that when he sang – sharanagat deenarth-paritraan paraayane, sarvasyaarti hare devi narayane namostute, 'Protector of those seeking refuge, annihilator of misery, oh Goddess Narayani, accept my salutations,' – not just men and women but even the waves of the azure pond began to dance. Fish would rise to the water's surface and splash around, while even the wind swinging on the keekar tree seemed to repeat the mantra.

But what can Laspandit say about those young lads with their burgeoning muscles? He blames the times we live in. How much has changed right in front of his eyes. Everything has been turned upside down. The arrival of TV and VCR in a village like Matan has meant that children have abandoned their books and the adults their satsang, those meetings devoted to discourses on ethical and religious matters, to stick glued to the TV till late at night. Laspandit feels sorry that children are growing up without imbibing the correct values. Not only are they disrespectful towards their elders, even their conversation has become boorish.

All day and night film songs like "*Ishq, ishq, ishq*" and "*Sala main to sahab ban gaya*" are on their tongues.

Earlier, Laspandit had tried to counsel the children occasionally. "Arre Maharaje! Is it not better to revise your school lesson instead of straining your eyes staying up watching TV at night? Instead of ornamenting each class for three years, isn't better to move on and offer hope to Jiya-Leela, your parents? Darbaridas..."

"Shiva- Shambho! What terrible times! All the time it's dhishum-dhishum, fighting and boxing... And what is this language you have begun to use, my lad? Abuses like sala, shit and my foot sprinkle every sentence. A tight slap on your behind will immediately teach you how to speak properly!"

The boys either ignored him or laughed and said, "Kaka, you go on with your Shivom. Just spare us. Why get mixed up with the young? We swear we will renounce the world and retire to the forest when we reach your age...". In short, "Old man your day is done. Don't bore us."

The truth is that Laspandit did chant Shiva-Shambho all his life – for his livelihood, as well as for his peace of mind. But everything has changed before his eyes. The youngsters who played gulli-danda and bat and ball have learnt to play with deadly metal toys. The whole mood of the valley has changed. Small children climb on the walls of their cowsheds and tease Laspandit, "The militants are coming, the militants are coming!" In the beginning, Laspandit admonished them, brandishing his fists, "Dhat! Ismail, you rumour-monger." But they just laughed and ran away. Soon, however, the young men began to follow suit and finally the day came when the spotless cloth that hung on Laspandit's shoulder was besmirched. It was fated that he be ruined, and so he was.

"The consequence of the misdeeds committed in past lives?" What else could it be? He had neither wished anyone ill nor harmed anybody in this one.

"Don't talk of good and evil deeds, Baba!" Laspandit's son Gasha, earlier a studious, sober and obedient boy, has become as aggressive as a monkey perched on a boulder these days, and keeps flaring up without reason. "Karma! The result of bad karma! Is that all? Is that the only lesson left for us to parrot? The lakhs of people going through hell, did all of them perform evil deeds in past lives? And those masters of our fates, the powerful ones, who can stoop to any level, commit any crime to protect their positions, what about the outcome of their karma? They are the ones responsible for our ruin..."

Gasha, aged twenty-five... quick, sharp-eyed, volatile... victim of the conflicts he has experienced and witnessed. He is not the only one embittered. A whole generation is seething. Homeless, landless, unemployed...helpless against the curse of living as a foreigner in one's own country! The skies did not come down all of a sudden. One does not turn into an enemy within a day. They are all pawns in a conspiracy.

To begin with there were minor skirmishes, then came the killings, rapes and arson. Then, the boys who passed them on the road began to look directly into their eyes and sing loudly, "We want Pakistan, without the Pandits but with the Panditanis, their women."

Gasha had warned his father that very day, "Baba, it is not safe to live here anymore. Anything can happen to us now."

But Laspandit did not agree. He believed in the shared heritage of Lal Dedi, Mahzoor, Azad, Habba Khatoon, and Master Jinda Kaul. He had always lent ear to that sweet melody in which no one was either a Muslim or a Hindu. All were children of that same God, the supreme father. And then he had never learnt to think about the inauspicious. Instead, he often narrated the story of the lost traveller to those who were inflicted with gloomy thoughts. "A traveller who was wandering in the forest sat down to rest under a big tree. Overcome with hunger, he began to think, ' If only somebody would come and give me two handfuls of rice that my exhausted frame would revive.' Lo and behold! A miracle occurred! In the blinking of an eye, a plate filled with delicious food appeared in front of him. After eating his fill, the traveller again thought, 'I wish I had a comfortable bed to sleep on.' Instantly, a soft, luxurious bed materialized. The man stretched out comfortably but a sudden fear raised its head. 'Such a dark night!' he thought. 'Such a lonely forest! What if a wild animal comes and attacks me?' Immediately, a hungry lion appeared and gobbled him up."

Narrating such stories, Laspandit was convinced that there do exist moments when we receive what we ask for. Some invisible power says 'tathastu', so be it, for every thought and desire. So, how and why could a person like Laspandit have thought of anything inauspicious!

But the inauspicious occurred – affected the whole community. Later, the whole valley was sucked in.

Sometimes women were dishonoured, at other times people found notices stuck to doors, threats were made. Friends and neighbours pleaded helplessly, "Go away to the plains for a while. The atmosphere has been ruined. No one even tries to understand. Come back as soon as the situation improves..."

But Laspandit did not budge till the catastrophe occurred. It happened like this: halfway through the night there was knocking on the door and four strangers entered, like calamity itself. Gasha tried to stop them but they were four – and fully armed. One blow was enough to fling him to the ground. Laspandit took off his turban and placed it at their feet. Shobhawati clutched their feet too and pleaded. But they twisted Jaya's arms and carried her away. Jaya, who cowered like a terrified pigeon. Agonized screams continued to pierce the stillness of the dark night for a long, long time...

After he returned to his senses, Gasha picked up his father like a sack of rice and dumped him in a truck. They locked their door and clutching a few bundles under their arms, set off. Without giving a thought to where, which way they were going. They dropped anchor at Trikuta Nagar in a shelter, a sarai where around twenty families had already taken refuge, each trying to turn an area as small as a duree into a dwelling place.

Since that day, Laspandit's thoughts have been neither auspicious nor inauspicious. Morning and evening he routinely washes the six strands of his sacred thread and chants the Gayatri Mantra – *Om bhuah bhurva svaha, tatsviturenyum, bhargo devasya dheemahi, dhiyu yu nah prachodayat.* He does not abandon his old practices. Hearing the mantra, Gasha loses his temper, "Matters did not deteriorate in a day. You elders hid your eyes and beaks in your wings – ostrich-like. Mindless beliefs, prayers that serve to direct brains only towards virtuous deeds! If you had only become alert in time..." Gasha has not become impertinent but he cannot come to terms with the situation. But then, has Laspandit himself been able to do so? What all should he be expected to forget...home and hearth, outer courtyard and inner rooms...the temple? Not just his ancestral inheritance, even his umbilical cord lies there, buried under the walnut tree. The cremation ground stretching out under the shade of the keekar and ved vriksha trees is counting the days as it waits for him with open arms. Immersed in eternal sleep his dear grandfather, father and mother must be searching for him out there. There is no release ever, from one's dust, one's land!

Gasha had spoken to Riyaz before the disaster occurred, "What should I do? Babba is just not ready to leave home and go anywhere."

Riyaz is his childhood friend – his companion in everything good and bad. He had bent his head, "Try to make Babba understand. I too am thinking of going away for a few days. Our troubles are no less. These people are divided into so many groups and gangs. Whom all can we save ourselves from?"

"But you? Why should you be afraid?"

"We are afraid, Gasha. Don't you know what happens to people who do not join their jehad? I don't want to get involved."

That very day Gasha had sensed the darkness that was gathering strength... But he was helpless in the face of Babba's obstinacy. Anyway, what would have been achieved even if he had managed to prevail? But it is impossible to prevent one's mind from striving to undo what has already occurred! What if this had happened, what if that...? Trading blame...the limits of exhaustion and desperation...

Laspandit and Shobhawati performed the tarpan, the ceremony for the dead, for Jaya. Day and night her mother grieved for her with heart-rending cries. Laspandit would put his palm over her mouth to stop her wailing. Was anyone happy here? There is no instrument that can measure the degrees of sorrow. It is just sorrow – nothing more, nothing less...dense...dark...impenetrable sorrow.

To listen, to see...there is no respite from this as long as one is in possession of one's senses. What reprieve do we have from life itself? Who knows whether Laspandit, with a wet towel wrapped around his head, sitting diffidently in the corner of a crowded minibus, thinks anything at all or merely sits there like a lump of clay, panting, jerking as the bus bumps its way. Who knows? The people around him glance contemptuously at the tilak marking his forehead. "Ai...ee pandit, move a bit! How much space will you take? Hunh! Anywhere you look, you find these people."

Laspandit shrinks like a snail. Dissolving in the salty gutter of his sweat in utter silence. Or perhaps, with his eyes closed, he has been transported to his village, where the tender blush of morn spreads like a soft red powder on the garland of snow-capped hills, and the wild mynahs burst into song when the east wind playfully teases them

– and melodiously trill – *teevee tut, teeve tut*! With a datun stick clutched in his teeth, Laspandit walks through the cool shade of the veer and keekar trees towards the blue fountain where the fish splash around, eagerly waiting for him to arrive with their feed.They rise to the surface of the water with open mouths and leap up to swallow the grain. After completing his morning routine he worships the sun, intoning – *Om mitraya namah! Om ravaye namah! Om*..."And the clients waiting for him! But what do people here know about him? What respect can one have for a stranger?

The bus conductor is shaking Laspandit, the last passenger. "Get up pandit? Will you sprawl here forever?"

Is somebody calling him? The hungry fish? Where are you? Where? Who is he? People surround him.

Must be a refugee! A migrant! Wherever you look, you find these people!

Poor things! How long will they rot in the camps? More than four years have gone by! In the beginning people were sympathetic to their suffering. But for how long? Schools, colleges, bazaars, and shops–are all overflowing. Wherever one looks one finds migrant camps, migrant shops, migrant schools...

How long can human beings put up with this? For how long can they tolerate other human beings?The government has plugged its ears. It just distributes rations. Keep filling this cavern of a stomach and keep rotting in the camps! Will we continue to live here for generations to come? Who knows?

"Arre! You think he may be dead? He is a skeleton, this old man..."

As soon as some water was sprinkled on his face, Laspandit opened his eyes and looked around dazed, "Arre! Where have I reached? I had to go to Gandhi Nagar! Today was the shraddha of Mattu saheb's father."

Here, even in exile, some well-to-do people of the community summoned Laspandit on the pretext of performing rituals and handed him ten or twenty rupees in return – along with some grain. After all, how many people are well versed in the shastras and puranas these days?

Laspandit walks a mile or two to save the bus fare. He buys some vegetables and other goods in the hope of protecting the sense of his own existence within and outside home. The skeletal remains of a withered bush...

Gasha teaches science in the school for displaced children. These days he goes around the offices for government relief and keeps hearing the word 'migrant' that has now become a term of abuse. His identity is slowly fading away like the valley's hangul, that special breed of deer, fast becoming extinct. Ceasing to exist is gradually becoming his destiny.

But Laspandit's companions in the shelter continue to count the days. Days...months...years. "We came in November 1989..." Deenanath hosiery-wala chants the same old tune, "My shop was crammed with goods, the latest stuff from Delhi and Punjab, I handed over the keys to Wali Mohammad. He is still a man of principles. I had believed that the situation would improve in a couple of months..." Leela's lamentations have no end – she's a heart patient. "My this...my that...! I had a toosh shawl especially woven for Lalli by Ali ju. All her dowry...where must it be now? Those huge ancestral vessels of bronze and brass – kandaals, degchis, the embroidered gabbas Anantnag is famous for. We had got Lhasa carpets all the way from Ladakh…and here our bodies have become all knotted up sleeping on bare mats. And still these people here call us beggars! Destitute!"

From morning to evening, Radhey Shyam, the retired teacher, searches for his home in the newspapers. His hands are still grimy – sand and dirt embedded in his nails. Who knows – it may have already been reduced to ashes – so many have already lost theirs to the flames.

It has become so important – for the people in the sarai – to read the newspaper.

Today such and such minister has gone on tour – to assess the situation.

Ten were killed today, six injured…a bomb exploded in Doda… They entered Pulwama from across the border, weapons have been seized…

Nityanand settles the cord tied to his spectacles behind his ear and lights a flame of hope. "The minister says that the situation is improving… Look…see what's written here?… Read it."

Two British citizens abducted.

"Sure…the improved situation! Fold it shut, close the newspaper! Let at least a flicker of hope live on." Heated breath rises like smoke and spreads around. However, the discussion on the existing situation does not end even after they put the newspaper away. Now skirmishes have begun to occur in Jammu too. Two militants with weapons have been arrested in the Chowk.

"Whose organisation is this? 'Harkat-ul-Ansar'? Hadn't heard this name earlier."

"Listen, why don't Amnesty International and other Human Rights Organisations from abroad come to the shelter for the displaced?"

It's difficult to get to know whether Laspandit heard the news. He never expresses his opinion. The peaks of Trikuta Hills are visible from an open window and he's gazing intently in that direction. The lights on the winding hill track look like a galaxy of twinkling stars as they glitter in the dark. Laspandit's palms come together in a namaskar – "*sharanagat deenarth-paritraan paraayane*" – Laspandit keeps mumbling these days. What can one do about old habits? The mantra for prevention of adversity! What misfortunes have you not already lived through, Laspandit?

Shobhawati, Babli, Gasha – all three of them are lying next to Laspandit. Shobha's sari has slid up above her calf. Her sweat-soaked blouse sticks to her body, almost invisible. The room is an open hall. Women are huddled close to each other, as if lying completely exposed under the naked sky! Whenever Laspandit went to anybody's house in the village, he would clear his throat as soon as he entered the veranda. The women inside should at least get time to arrange their bodies into more modest postures and cover their heads before his gaze lights on them.

Laspandit gently spreads a corner of the bed sheet over Shobha's breasts. It would be good if she could get some sleep. Forget her sorrows for some time. She has not slept for several nights. Awake or asleep, she starts up suddenly and begins to scream, "Who's there? Don't open the door.

Those people will come again… You scoundrels! Stop twisting my child's wrists! They will get bruised…"

Babli's right arm has slipped into Babba's lap. Laspandit searches his memory – is there any mantra to check attachment? Babli has grown from ten years to fourteen, here in the shelter. Both the generous and the greedy – their mouths watering – turn up on the pretext of offering sympathy and assistance. Shobha cannot hide her maturing daughter away in her womb. She ties her budding breasts tightly with a piece of cloth.

Laspandit does nothing at all. He just keeps watching, keeps listening – as if he were deaf and dumb. He does not even lose his cool. Has he finally forgotten the mantra that keeps trouble away?

He is pushed around as he stands for hours in the queue for rations. When his turn comes, he puts his bag in front of the man distributing them, only to hear putrid words that enter his ears like molten lead, "Aaee!… Old man! Why do you come to get the rations? You'll be squashed flat by this hungry mob one day. Why don't you send your daughter?"

"Yes, yes, she is young. Just send her. You will get the rations fast, and good stuff too!"

The volunteer laughs, exposing his yellow teeth and nudges Laspandit. The wheat spills, grains spread on the muddy ground. Laspandit quietly begins to gather it up. You glutton! Laskaak! You, who would generously feed dogs with half of the freshly cooked rice you were eating… and these so called government appointed helpers… Are they any better than the militants? Jaya was swallowed up by one kind of terror. It's approaching Babli now in a new form… O Lord Vishnu! Where is your chakra, the wheel on your finger that destroys sinners? Why have you become so weak? Powerless Laspandit! Powerless gods! The powerless guardians of the country! Each is deaf to the other's cry!

Pain pierces the back of his head like a sharp spear. How brutally those people had knocked him down. But for the swampy ground under the mulberry tree, his skull would have cracked into pieces. Laspandit wonders, Does Phata gwalin, Shabbir's mother, know about her son's doings? She probably does not. He's sure she doesn't! She used to say, "Pandit, don't come to get milk in such bitter weather. Yard deep snow and such biting cold! Your death will be on my head if you suddenly pop off in this freezing weather. Is Shabbo not your son too? He will deliver the milk to your house…"

True, he was his son…but…! His mind stops functioning. Laspandit gets entangled in the maze of 'ifs' and 'buts' and loses his voice. He had failed to preserve the dignity of his turban, his honour. Has he just been chanting mantras?… Pointless mantras, devoid of worthy action?

But the wait continues. He does not forget anything. The fragrance of home and village is still sharp in his nostrils despite the passage of years. The taste of lotus stem from Manasbal and water chestnuts from Vooler is still fresh on the tip of his tongue. The wait for the frugal meals of daal-roti, is merely a means of killing time. There, soft snowflakes must be knocking at the closed windows and not seeing them around, forcing their way in through cracks and fissures, to enter and drench the desolate beds.

They ponder...The refugees continue to wait. The newspaper continues to be studied. The hunt through national and international reports for that tiny bit of information upon which hinges all their hope of returning home! But the news items throw cold water on their hopes.

Here it is! Breaking news... Qazi Sahib murdered!... A procession of lakhs of people!... Slogans of Pakistan Murdabad, down with Pakistan!... Shiva! Shiva! Is there anything left for Laskaak to say?

The commentary follows the news. And the pages of history continue to turn. Six centuries ago. Is it really true that history repeats itself?

The inhabitants of the sarai are hopeful. We resettled in the past, we will settle once again. It's better – hope provides one with strength to continue living.

Late in the night – a moonless night. A soft, nervous step is heard on the steps of the sarai. The commentary comes to a halt. Each hair turns into an ear – Who-oo-o? Terror-stricken people get alarmed at the most absurd things! "Who's there?" The sackcloth curtain trembles in response. A fair hand moves the curtain a bit.

Does Laspandit live here? Laspandit from Matan?

A weary, thin voice rises and halts. Why did it feel as if a boat had suddenly overturned in the Dal Lake? Gulp! It's all quiet elsewhere.

A silence teeming with doubts and questions... Or is it peace? The peace that descends before or after the storm? At that time too, Laspandit was staring at the twinkling, twisting path going up the Trikuta Hills. God bless Jagmohan! Now the pilgrimage to the Vaishno Devi temple can take place through the night too…

"Laskaak, someone is looking for you," Deenanath and Nityanand, both spoke out together. Suspicious voices, suspicious gazes! Who could it be? Who would come so late at night? Shobhawati rose mechanically, like a rubber doll. Babli and Gasha too.

Yes, it's her… Eyes almost scrubbed out, the same lotus flower peeping through the crumpled head covering. And in her arms? Is it a baby? He Ram! Whose child is it?

"Yo-ou!" Shobhawati screamed. Had she seen a ghost in the dark?

"Yes Kaakani, it's me!" The shadow holding the baby leapt towards Shobhawati's voice, trampling the feet of a few children and adults.… Aah, oh! The girl's body began to tremble with suppressed grief. Babli and Gasha embraced their sister! Laspandit – shocked and stunned – just continued to stare.

Hai ma! Oh supreme goddess! This Jaya… How did she manage to leave your abode and reach here? We had taken her for dead. We even performed her tarpan ceremony! Shiva, Shiva!

The whole camp has become alert in the meantime. Who? How? With whom? Questions showered like rain. Who gave her this address?

Aah! A sharp pain pierced Jaya's leg. Something had pierced her foot in the dark. The border of her odhani, tied around it, was drenched in fresh blood. When she put the child – a baby girl – down, she began to whimper soundlessly, her throat parched. Quick, short, gasps shook the tiny skeleton of bones. An electric shock went through Laspandit. He rose suddenly and came back with a glass of water from the clay pot on the shelf. He handed the glass to Jaya, and taking a little water in his cupped hand, took it to the child's lips. *Poch-poch*! The baby made tiny sounds as she sucked in the water. Who knows for how long she had not eaten? The inside of her mouth was all cracked. Laspandit picked up the baby and began to pat her. He was as oblivious of the threatening questions springing out of the crowd that had gathered around him, as of Shobhawati's ceaseless lamentation. If he could get some milk from somewhere, or honey…but where could he find honey here? Nityabhai is in the habit of drinking tea every morning. He might have some milk…

But Jaya could not escape the questions: "No, I am alone. Ran away from the hospital. A nurse helped me there. Put me on a truck. I have been wandering around searching for two days. In different camps, Geeta Bhavan, then here… Each and every joint is aching. I'm totally drained out."

"Those people had taken her, isn't it? They will come here looking for her. No, this girl can't live here. We too have families."

"No! No! Nobody saw me running away. And anyway he is dead. Died in an internal clash." 'He' was probably the father of the child.

But the people's suspicions could not be quelled, probably never would.

"No, they cannot be trusted. We too have women in the family. Send her away."

"I am completely exhausted. Let me stay. I have suffered so much," Jaya's voice was smothered by her sobs.

"Bhaya, what crime has the girl committed? Who has remained untouched in this dreadful storm? Some have been robbed, others injured. Have pity!"

But the terror-struck crowd would not revoke its decision – "Laspandit, how can you of all people say this? You who have spoken the language of dharma all your whole life? Will you embrace this bundle of sin in this time of distress? No, we need to protect the honour of our women. If you want, you may take her and look for shelter elsewhere."

Laspandit felt as if a swarm of wasps had stung him. It was after years that the people in the camp heard his voice, raised to the highest pitch. "Don't talk of honour. My honour was lost the day they trampled my dastaar under their shoes. What is left of your honour anyway? What honour remains of people like you who stand in queues waiting for titbits like beggars and refuse to budge even after being kicked like dogs? And don't even mention dharma. You are not following any dharma by driving out an unfortunate daughter who has come seeking shelter. Laspandit may have lost his honour but he still understands what dharma means…"

Laspandit has gone crazy…but how can they agree to chop off their own necks? They wish to live on.

Jaya wept till she had no tears left but Shobhawati's mourning would not end. "We had even performed the shraddha for this ill-fated girl." Gasha remained quiet and did not embrace her. Was it because she was a sinner? Or was it because they could not have continued to stay in the sarai with her and did not have the means to move out and rent a room? Moreover, no one would be willing to rent them any room after discovering Jaya's past. "You should have left the baby there," he said softly, "it was a serious mistake to bring her with you." Jaya looked up at her brother and felt that her own brother – born of the same womb – had humiliated her once again. Shoved a rusted knife into her heart.

"She is my child, a part of me – as wretched as me. How could I have abandoned this blameless creature, brother?" Did these words emerge or get smothered within her?

Jaya wiped her eyes. She gathered the baby in her arms. How wounding it is to be humiliated by one's own flesh and blood.

Jaya got up to leave and Laspandit tried to stop her. "No, no! Where will you go with this innocent babe?" Shobhawati had perhaps fainted away after beating her breast in anguish. Babli was sobbing uncontrollably. Gasha – his head bent low – stood like a criminal. Jaya clung to her father, "Babba! Don't grieve. Just pray for me!"

Jaya dragged herself down the stairs with defeated steps. And the prayer clamoured within Laspandit, the mantra that staved off disaster – *Sharanagat Deenarth...Sharanagat Deenarth*.

Laspandit turned towards the window and the other people in the shelter vanished into their own spaces. There was nothing more left for them to say!

Who knows whether they managed to sleep through the night or kept awake, who knows when Shobhawati recovered consciousness and for how long Gasha cursed himself for the words he had uttered? In the meantime, the night spent itself hour by hour. When the darkness melted, the people in the shelter noticed that Laspandit had vanished. A search began. Had he gone to relieve himself? Maybe he had gone to bathe in the river Tawi. But his bedding, the bundles of his belongings had disappeared too. Arre! Where could he have gone?

Could he have followed the girl? He had become crazy anyway. He would certainly die before his time! That's certain! Would those people ever spare him?

People said whatever came into their heads at the moment. But the truth was the manner in which Laspandit vanished brought their shame to life all over again.

*Translated by Vibha S. Chauhan*

# *Homeless in the Cantonment*

*Alpana Mishra*

Whatever is happening outside happens as if in sleep. Whatever happens in sleep seems as though lost outside. Searching for what has been lost, I potter about here and there. Household chores engage the body; they don't engage the mind. The mind acts so strangely. I think of sunning the clothes. When I open the wardrobe, his clothes catch my eye first. His suits, pants, shirts, ties, belts, old name tabs, some stars, berets hung up…all seem to smell of something like him. I stand there rooted. He who created such a commotion before leaving, has gone, leaving a vacant space – as if something extremely essential has been removed from life.

No, I can't remain standing here. I have things to do. The children have gone to school; it'll be better if I'm done with airing the clothes before they come back. It's sunny today. This town is pretty unreliable when it comes to sun and clouds. I carry the clothes to the back yard. There are some plastic chairs scattered around. I spread the heavier clothes on the chairs and the lighter ones on the clothesline.

I hear the sound of a car. Emerging out of the past, a red Maruti is heading towards our house. A new car. I run to the window. The car stops in front of our house. The door opens and a handsome young man alights – tall, dusky, with a moustache that adds charm to his face. He is wearing a cap. He doesn't wear this kind of a cap usually. He could be questioned about it. His head is tonsured. He isn't taking the cap off. It is like a helmet to him.

The door on the other side opens and a slender girl alights. The doors behind open with a bang. Two small children jump out – as if marigold blossoms have turned into balls. As if they have been filled with air and can only bounce. The slender girl runs and stops the bouncing balls from crashing into each other.

That slender girl is Mrs Kumar. Till recently, folks often called her 'Meenu', but her husband's new position has ensured that she is referred to only as Mrs Kumar. The habit has taken root and now if some old acquaintance happens to call her Meenu, it makes her cringe as though she had been reminded of some forgotten person, someone recalled from the dead.

Mrs Kumar is holding two bottles of water so the balls can be given water at the same time without getting into a scuffle over it. She's reached the door and has stopped there. The door is padlocked. They don't know that there is a window in the room beyond this door through which I am watching them and will continue to watch this scene even after they have exited from it. I will keep watching it. Rewind and watch it again and again. The handsome young man tosses the bunch of keys to Mrs Kumar who catches it deftly. She smiles faintly. Seeing her smile the handsome young man smiles too, in his mind. Outwardly, he looks unhappy though. He tells the children – "You go in first." They have entered the room now.

I can see you, Mrs Kumar. I watch myself. I see you're the sad face that is mine. You may smile at Major Kumar all you want; never again will that mischievous twinkle appear in those eyes. Why can't you accept you are sad like Major Kumar?

"In the army you are not allowed to tonsure your head," someone says.

"But we have our own rituals," the young man says mildly.

"Who was it?" someone asks without asking.

"Father." He tells them without speaking.

"Wear a topi, a beret or cap in the office. No one will know."

He feels sad. Why shouldn't anyone know of his father's death? Of course, he had mentioned it in his application for leave. Everyone knows it but still he must hide, himself, his home too.

In the army, home is one's wife and children. A father is not included in one's home. He is part of one's native village. Whatever town he may be in, it is considered the native village. Everyone's parents are far away, that is, in the native village. We may visit the native village; we cannot bring it here. Even if we do, it can be only for a few days. And were we to insist that the native village stay with us, it will feel bored. Will insist that it wants to go back to where it came from. Folks will say, "They have 'guests'," or, "Their 'guests' left." He has never heard of anyone's parents dying in the cantonment, never seen folks busy organizing a funeral – shrouds and bamboos, family acquaintances waiting to place their shoulders under the bier. The headache of getting hold of priests etc.

"Hmm," he says.

He doesn't say, "So many problems have arisen back home."

Nor does he say, "Someone passing away unsettles one's life so much, like water churned up. It takes time for it to settle."

He only says, "Hmm," which could mean anything. Even something like, "We will see."

The girl Meenu is busy, hurriedly putting the house into some semblance of order.

She is missing bhaiyya, their orderly. He would have been a big help in packing. He has already left. Who could have foreseen that everything would happen so suddenly? That he would have to leave so suddenly? For both places. His father's death and the summons for the Kargil war would happen simultaneously. The unit has received moving orders. Meenu is flitting from the kitchen to the bedroom, from the children to her husband, from the stuff brought back from the village to the stuff to be packed for Major Kumar.

Major Kumar is silent.

"Here take this. Put his clothes on." Deliberately Mrs Kumar hands the younger son to him. Along with his clothes and the tin of talc.

How can one remain frozen in any moment of existence? One has to come out of such moments. All such moments have to be traversed.

Major Kumar has powdered the bouncing child and is now struggling to dress him.

"Why do you worry? Everything will be done by the morning. Just double-check your kit – the BPT backpack and all your uniforms. DMS boots, hunter shoes etc…" Mrs Kumar will remind him.

"Hmm." Major Kumar will be heard saying, which can be interpreted in several ways. Even 'I don't feel up to it'. He will unpack the backpack and checking all its contents, will put everything back. Now he will live in his combat uniform. And he will start attending to the combat uniform.

Mrs Kumar is laying food on the table. Her two flower balls have bounced so much all day that they are sleepy now. Mrs Kumar is coaxing them to eat but they don't want to.

"Don't bother them. Let them be," Major Kumar tells her, attaching the name-tabs to his uniform.

Mrs Kumar abandons her attempt to feed the children. Lifting the younger one, who is asleep, off the sofa, she glances at Major Kumar. Major Kumar is not looking at her or he would have picked up the child himself.

"Should I bake you a cake? To take with you?"

Mrs Kumar is back in the kitchen. She calls out from

there. In such a loud voice as if Major Kumar were far off. Very far. At the Pakistan border. At the very Line-of-Control.

"No."

Major Kumar speaks as softly as if she were close by. Right next to him, or leaning on his shoulder.

"You are so brave."

She doesn't know when Major Kumar came in to stand behind her, very close.

"I am not crying." Mrs Kumar doesn't turn around.

Major Kumar touches her shoulder gently, and she turns and hides her face in his chest. Major Kumar encircles her in a tender embrace. Now no one will speak.

I am struggling to learn to drive the red Maruti. He had taught me to start the car and change the gears in a hurry. In the beginning, armed with that skill, I used to move the car back and forth. Now I am a little more confident. I am trying to drive out and make a turn.

"If I had had the time I would have..."

"Turned me into an expert driver, no?" I know what he's about to say.

This car had been bought just before Pitaji passed away. After that so many things happened so fast. Major Kumar was summoned to Kargil. Only it doesn't feel as if he has really left. Yes, he isn't around at the moment. It is as if has just left to go close by, around the corner. Will be back – any moment. The house is exactly as he left it. Even the muddy prints of his shoes remain on the floor. Old? Not really. Just dried by the wind and heat. I don't allow them to be swabbed away. No, I don't think it looks dirty. Earlier, when

Major Kumar was around, I thought marks on the floor looked dirty. Innumerable must have been the times when I told him not to walk in with dirty shoes, use the back entrance. But he always forgot and would get embarrassed the moment he saw the marks of his feet on the floor.

"Oh, ho!" he would say, then, "Forget it."

"Who do you think will wipe these all day?"

He would laugh carelessly. And now I want to hoard those very same footprints.

What am I doing standing here thinking, with the ADM Branch letter in my hand? Major Kumar has only been gone fifteen days and we have to gather up our lives and leave this place. Where will we go? Not far. Right here within the cantonment. Into two rooms. I am not the only one who has to move. Many other women like me will be moving. We will all have to leave shoe-prints behind.

The ADM Branch writes – "The families of officers posted to the field are in surplus. There are not enough houses. Our priority is to allot houses to officers returning from field duty. We are allotting you two rooms till you can find rented accommodation in the civilian area. There is a long list of applicants for Separated Family Accommodation. You are 174th on that list. We will inform you as soon as Separated Family Accommodation becomes available. You may shift to the civilian area directly if you so desire."

Mrs Verma is adamant, "How can we move to two rooms just like that? We won't leave till the academic session comes to an end. My husband is at the front and you are asking us to leave the house at this time?"

"The CO's family hasn't been asked to shift," someone points out angrily.

The Admin Officer has come personally. He tries to explain sheepishly, "What are we to do Ma'am? Right now there is a surplus of families. Officers who have served in the field for three, five and six years also need houses. They will be our priority. We can accommodate only officers posted here. We will see to it that you aren't inconvenienced. We will send some jawans to help with the shifting."

"There are no kitchens there. The rooms are too small. Where will we keep our stuff? And what about parking?"

"In that case you could move to Ghanghoda. The old bungalows there could be repaired..."

"Ghanghoda? Oh God! How will our children commute to school?"

"In that case ma'am, you'd better shift to the rooms being offered, and look for a decent civilian accommodation in the meantime."

Civilian lodgings! No, no! We are better off in the two-roomed accommodation. Mrs Verma sits undecided.

I agree.

We will convert those two tiny rooms into home. We will partition one room with our almirahs and turn it into a small drawing room and a small kitchen. The gas stove can sit on top of a wooden box; we will do the dishes in the bathroom. Two cots joined together could make do for a double bed. We will manage somehow. Most of our stuff, specially the glassware and china we use for parties, showpieces, mementoes can be packed away in boxes...

We have set up house in the two rooms allotted to us.

These are old rooms behind the mess. Rows of rooms that form an almost square neighbourhood. There is a flat space in the middle with some desolate looking bushes. They must have been planted long ago. They look abandoned. So, we are here. And many like us. We have named our locality the J.J. Colony or Jhuggi-Jhonpri colony. There are lots of children. They make this slum a lively place. No need to go to the distant park. The children are there and so is the open space. The children play in the space under our watchful gazes. The communal veranda in front of the rooms could have provided room for a few cars but that would mean obstructing the passage. So the scooters and cars have been parked right in front of the rooms. We too, bought a cover for our red Maruti. We exchange driving tips with each other and are turning into competent drivers. Mrs Ramachandran has begun to drive expertly. Maybe someday, someone will say that about me too.

We are all searching for somewhere to stay in the civilian area. We cannot afford very expensive houses. We only have our husbands' salaries to fall back upon. In this town, most people have constructed an extra room on the terrace to rent to students; it brings some extra income and security. Searching for a house in the civilian part is like stepping into another world for us. Folks want to know if we know somebody reliable who can vouch for strange women like us so they can feel reassured letting out their accommodation. We have no standing on our own. We can vouch for each other; that is all. But as soon as a husband is back from the field or his unit moves, the wife and family will vanish. They cannot stay behind just to keep the others company.

Folks in the civil area know this and so feel obliged to ask us for references.

Undeterred, we continue our forays into town. After the children leave, we cook hurriedly and leave. We are home before they get back. In the evening too, while the children play, we are on our rounds again. We return after a couple of hours. Unsuccessful. We want to write to each of the house-owners to construct their houses in such a manner so there is a corner for the family of a man gone to war. We cannot write to the government. It will jeopardize our men's jobs. Many of the husbands have cleared the Staff College. A bright future awaits them, once they are back from the front. Women overlook their own problems for the sake of their husbands.

A couple of us go to check the S.F. twice a week. The waiting list has remained unchanged for a month. It could take up to a year. Houses are expected to fall vacant only if a unit moves to a peace station. Our husbands are aware that we have been forced to vacate our houses and dumped in two rooms or even one, according to their ranks. And yet when they call we must say, "Everything is fine here. Don't worry about us."

Amma hasn't been keeping well ever since Pitaji passed away. I want to bring her here to us so she can get better care. Because of the children's education I can't shift to the village. Major Kumar's younger brother has been unemployed for a long time and is into drugs now. He cannot be relied upon. His sister has problems with her in-laws and could go back to the parental home any day. The eldest sister is unable to do anything for her mother. She is married to an extremely busy software engineer and has to shoulder a lot of responsibilities for her own family. So I will somehow have to fetch Amma.

Obviously, we haven't found a house so far. Mrs Reddy has found one and will be shifting soon, I've heard. She is in a row of rooms some distance away. I haven't found anything. Mrs Sharma next door and Mrs Mishra haven't found accommodation either. Adm. Branch has sent a letter again. Two months have passed. We have another month to find accommodation, failing that we will have to pay a damage rent according to square feet – ten thousand rupees for these two rooms. Baap re! We can't afford that sort of rent. We cannot believe they would actually deduct that sum. Our husbands are fighting at the front for the country, how can they take more than half their salaries as rent?

I am on an all-out mission to find suitable rented accommodation.

Someone spoke of a house near the Ballupur crossroad and I am headed there. There is a crowd at the crossroads. I am holding on to my two flower balls tight.

"Mamma, what's going on there?" The younger one is curious.

"What's going on?" I too want to know.

A three-ton army truck carrying a coffin draped in the national flag. Some jawan's body from Kargil. The Gorkha Rifles, local boys, have a long list of casualties. Almost every other house is mourning a man lost to war. I stand stunned, holding my bouncy balls. Someone speaks of the newly married Premnagar lad whose body arrived in a similar manner the other day, "People heaped his coffin with flowers."

"Who is dead, Mamma?" The younger one wants to know.

The older one has sensed something. He understands the significance of the three-tonner. He is scared.

"Someone from our army...I will tell you at home." He tells his brother to quieten him.

"OK."

Clutching my sons' hands I almost run. Suddenly, the forces look like so many sacrificial goats: well-fed, decorated.

How long can a goat's mother rest assured? The driver of the three-ton is asking someone for directions.

Pakistan has returned the mutilated body of a lieutenant. Air Force pilot Nachiketa has been successful in his mission. Colonel Narayanan has not been able to fetch any white rajmah for me from the Dras sector. He had assured me, "I will definitely send you some, ma'am."

His body too, must have been carried to his faraway home. We didn't even know when. A handsome captain who used to play the mouth organ has become a martyr and a symbol of bravery. A young lieutenant who made sketches of Param Veer Chakra award winning martyrs has joined their ranks. He has been wiped out along with his art. The martyred body of Major Bisht is being brought to his hometown Uttarkashi. There has been a blast in the convoy in front of Major Sharma's vehicle. One officer, two JCOs, five NCOs dead on the spot....

The Prime Minister is addressing the nation from the ramparts of the Red Fort. Mathematicians have been called to calculate the exact age of the freedom of the country. Who are these folk braving the pouring rain, listening to the Prime Minister with rapt attention? There are others standing hidden under umbrellas. When did this country grow so many umbrellas? The tricolour has been unfurled in schools. The children chorus – *"Jan gan man adhinayk jaya he..."* On this special day the PA system of a temple is blaring out a patriotic film song instead of a bhajan – *"Mere desh ki dharati...."*

The soap bar is wrapped in the tricolour. The more patriotic you are the more soap bars you will buy. A major automobile manufacturer has come out with a new range of cars in the different colours of the national flag... Outside the Red Fort a police jawan has taken his officer hostage. Terrorists have created a minefield stretching from the native village to Delhi. People are walking on it. Those who matter, fly...The air is heavy with the sound of a worldwide dirge. The newspapers and magazines are busy extracting contributions in the names of the martyrs from the public...

The sister of a martyr is trying to immolate herself in front of the leaders. The government has allotted a petrol-pump in her brother's name, which is being run by some government lackey who insults the martyr's family when they demand money...

"What are the rules of the Defence Ministry?" I wish to ask a senior officer.

"We are not sure ma'am," the officer will say.

"Why not? Don't you have a family?"

"I'll find out and let you know, ma'am. Don't you worry."

What will he tell me? That the army doesn't give jobs to soldiers' widows? That they receive some money in exchange for husbands…a little more for officers, a little less for jawans. And who manages to get hold of that money? Those whose families can run around to claim it. Just them, isn't it? When it's so hard for us – what happens to the families of the jawans? Who is the war for? Why are our men fighting this war? For whose benefit? Whose peace? What is happening to the families left behind?

How many families had just one son who managed to get a job, now he too is gone. I have never been this troubled about life in the army before. Had never thought about my own future in the context of war. I used to think the war will come at some other time, but now it is war every day, hostages taken every day, casualties and martyrs every day….

"We should find jobs," I told my neighbour.

"We should find both – jobs and houses."

"Any information?"

"The phone lines have been down for a week now."

"Phones have become our life-lines."

"The lines might open today."

"They have to be careful, but still the families need to be informed…"

"They must be trying."

"Yes. They must be."

The phone lines have been down for the last fifteen days. We haven't been able to establish any contact with them. The phone lines have been cut as a precaution. If only I could just get the news that all is well from somewhere.

Mrs Sharma has a visitor; a jawan from their unit has brought her news.

Would he know how Major Kumar is doing?

We are past the notice date to vacate the rooms. Early in the morning a phone call brought news of Amma's death. I am leaving for the village with the children. Day before yesterday, news arrived from the front that some officers would be granted leave. Major Kumar is also expected to be back. He can proceed to the village as soon he comes. I can't wait for his arrival at this point. I am needed in the village to organize Amma's last rites. I have to go. I am busy getting ready, along with the children. I am going to need some cash too. I am busy adding and subtracting. At this time, can anything compensate for Major Kumar's absence? After fifteen days, suddenly a message from Major Kumar's brigade.

"What is it?" Mrs Sharma has crept from her room towards mine.

"If he is coming, why not wait for a day, Meenu? You will be all alone in the village." She is genuinely concerned.

"Hmm." I say like Major Kumar. It could mean anything, even 'pointless talk'.

"He is untraceable...was on patrol duty...two jawans missing with him..." After a long time, I say to myself.

Mrs Sharma grabs the wall for support before I do.

She will say something like, "So you go. Leave the children with me."

In the village folks will say something like, "We will pray for him."

*Translated by Madhu B. Joshi*

# There is Nothing Romantic at All

*Manisha Kulshreshta*

Nothing is truly romantic... Then how is one to create a romantic story?

Remember that day – when it had been just a week since your arrival? How I had adored that contemplative manner of yours. Eyes closed, you were sitting cross-legged on a mattress spread on the floor. Your pen was lying open amidst sheets of paper strewn all over. Your spectacles were in your pocket. I was to serve you a plateful of snacks with a mug of coffee, and then climb down the spiral stairs, without disturbing you. I had known then that a new story was taking birth. I was extremely curious and wanted to ask what the subject of this story would be. For quite some time you had not written anything on love. So, was it about love? Long before you visited this place, Achchan had given me your stories to read and according to him they were terrifyingly romantic. I was astounded at your portrayal of love, your depiction of the physical...also at the intensity of your tortured and tormenting romanticism!

There was a black and white picture of you on the gatefold of your book. An unusual face, with a non-Indian cast. Spiky hair. Your light coloured eyes could somehow be discerned even in that black and white picture. My father's words had awakened a simple, spontaneous curiosity: read this if you wish to see creative sensitivity at its pinnacle. The density of language and the complexity of the theme appear to challenge as well as complement each other in a way.

I could only understand Achchan's words partially. But, these stories did surprise me. Extraordinary stories about human connections, depicting the fluid and ever-changing psychology of man-woman relationships in a novel manner; narratives portraying an intensity of commitment in associations society declares immoral or illicit. In each story you demonstrated that there was no such thing as morality or immorality in love. Love was indeed, an absolutely legitimate experience.

Today, you, Malay, are creating a story right in front of me. I am dying of curiosity, but know that it is useless to enquire what it is going to be like. I will not ask. I have decided that I will not touch the bird's egg. If a naughty child touches an egg, the mother bird often abandons it and hurls it down from the nest. This is what my mother told me when I was small. During those mischief-filled afternoons, the thrilling moments when I would stealthily climb the table, then a chair placed on top of it, and peep at the eggs in the sparrow's nest in the skylight. I would pick up the brown-grey dotted eggs in my hands, keep turning them over and over for ages. Bring them close to my ears to find out if any sound, some tiny squeaks perhaps were emanating from them. Many a time, I would find the eggshells on the floor the next day, with their yellow and white liquid splattered about. I would feel miserable then, and vow never to touch them again. Yet, the very next day an overpowering urge would compel me to break the pledge.

At that time, you looked like that broody bird. Eyes shut. Oblivious of your surroundings. Deep in concentration, focused on creating a new cosmos around you. Unyielding, illuminated. Weighted with the pleasurable pain of giving birth. My curiosity kept simmering, kept me on the boil.

Words. Words. Words. That you write only to forget, while awestruck readers like me remain trapped in them for ages, keep drifting aimlessly in their unfathomable depths. What else? Definitely nothing else connected us at that time – other than the golden threads of that bridge of words. The words seemed to melt when I read them, trickle down on me drop by drop. On a clean cold floor, I would spread these words. They would scatter like drops of mercury. But once dispersed, was it easy to collect them again?

Your characters have strange names. From which forest have you gathered Saimbal, Mahua, Kasturi, Kewra, Kinsuk and Palash? Indeed, gleaned from your nomadic wanderings amidst old jungle forts and bone-dry trunks of trees, your narratives are like warped and crooked roots sculpted into fascinating images.

I had seen, from the branches of the jackfruit tree as it spreads around the staircase of the courtyard, the white translucent lace curtain on the window of your room moving slowly. I could spot your silhouette behind the curtain. It appeared as if your broad shoulders carried the burden of some unidentified pain. You were squeezing your lips between your thumb and index finger. Your eyes were inert, half closed. I could not make out the colour of your eyes. But this colour was spreading and tinting the sky.

How fortunate I was! I could actually witness the gestation of the new story of a popular storyteller. I heaved a sigh and just then, you looked up. There was nothing but apathy in your eyes. It pulled me in the way a black hole, full of myriad mysteries would. I hurried down. There was something haunting in your eyes. My moving image seemed to become motionless in the dilated pupil of your eye. Had you drunk too much last night?

Those days, you were strange. Ambivalent, irate and easily excitable. Often you would place things somewhere, forget about them and later get annoyed with Raghu. Your taste buds had lost all sensation those days. Uncomplainingly, you would devour anything and everything, almost like a pregnant woman! You would see and still not see me. I was surprised that you had not even eaten your breakfast today: south Indian garbage (this is what you have been calling our food).

You had still not caught sight of my moving frame. I know you did not deliberately ignore me. You just did not see me. I decided not to chide you about your uneaten breakfast. It was better not to express disapproval. Anyway, I too was getting late for college. All the way in the rickshaw, I kept thinking about you. These days, why are you so strange?

My father is also a writer but he remains normal. While writing, he often gets up to sort out affairs with the tenant. Does not hesitate to offer a stinging, sarcastic reply to Amma's grumbling. Responds to the vegetable vendor's yells by negotiating with him and buying vegetables. And you – you seldom emerge from your room. Yes, at night, dear writer, I catch you sneaking out. When you quietly descend the wooden staircase at the back, pass through the coconut grove; head for the city though the small wooden gate. You see, I have been familiar with the creaking of the wooden staircase since Ranjan Ammaran's time!

I have noticed many a time, how you abandon your pyjamas on the floor – two gaping holes almost like twin nests! Raghu and I have implicit instructions to not disturb these pyjamas so that if and when you return from roaming the narrow, gloomy lanes of this city or from some cheap bar or pub in a drunken state, you will have no difficulty sliding your legs into them, tying the string and collapsing on the bed like a chopped trunk of a tree.

I came back from college but did not see you. Not even at the dining table at night. Exhausted, fed up, Kinna had sent you food upstairs. I distinctly remember that you left your room around eleven that night. I could estimate your goings on from the room below. Had you delivered or not? What would the newborn story look like? How much did it weigh, was it pretty and healthy? Would it enchant everyone with one look? I lay awake all night in the room below trying to guess. Stillness, a dense silence pervaded it. You had not returned till then. While I waited, I read an old book of yours, published in 1984. It throbbed with idealism. When my doubts, my questions multiplied, your words became my last refuge. Just like the questionnaire in the initial pages of Tulsidas's *Ramcharit Manas*, in which, if you count eight squares from the point where your questing fingers halt and put the letters together, the words that form thus connecting letters will make a doha which will provide the solution to your problems. To answer the question of why you were so indifferent towards me, I closed my eyes and placed my finger inside the middle pages of your book on those cold, ineffably detached words and actually found answers – I believe people who love most intensely are the ones who appear silent and indifferent. Also, I have never believed age differences can come in the way of true love.

The wooden staircase was creaking gently. You were back. I wanted to stop you and ask if you were a remnant of the old generation of writers or some intermediary link.

You write incredible and distinctive stories. Where can one find such uninhibitedly penniless writers nowadays, solitary and impecunious, sponging off others for their drinks and wandering about on borrowed money?

Then suddenly I heard your shoe fall...and then the second, with a louder sound. You are quite uncivilized. Somebody stays beneath your room, Mr Writer.

That day, you had surfaced in our city out of the blue – almost like a solitary migratory bird that had strayed from an unknown country and descended on the old historic lake of a foreign land. Without a phone call or even a telegram. You did not even take the trouble to pen down two lines on a postcard. It was so upsetting for Amma. I had just got up from the doorstep, was dusting the rangoli from the free end of my pawada, when an auto rickshaw stopped there. You quarrelled with the auto rickshaw driver, in Hindi and English alternately. I intervened then.

"I have to meet Mr Nayar." You spoke in accent free English. Your captivating voice was slowly soaking in the humid air of Cochin.

"I am his daughter." You were surprised to hear a Malayali speak Hindi, that too in a non-Mallu accent.

"Maheshji has sent me here from Delhi. He gave this letter." For about five minutes you kept fumbling, searching for the letter in your pockets. And yes, a bunch of keys and a near empty wallet did fall down on the road

Several inquisitive faces had begun to peep from the neighbouring doors and windows.

"You can show that to Achchan. Come inside first." You didn't allow me to carry the meagre luggage you had: a small suitcase and handbag.

By then Achchan had appeared.

"Oh! So you are Malay? It is my good fortune that you have come here. Mahesh called last night." You looked at me with a peculiar expression of relief, which almost conveyed – so what if the letter can't be found, at least the phone call came.

My heart missed a beat. So, this was Malay…from whose stories I had made my friends read underlined excerpts! You bloody sadist! This is what I would mutter after reading your stories and looking at your picture on the gatefold of the book. You looked different in your picture, smiling, but in person you surprised me. How could this frosty-faced, cruel-looking person write such stories?

"I am not a temporary visitor but will stay for a long time."

"Kindly let the auto driver go." Achchan had to pay even for the auto.

How could you have paid such a hefty bill? You had made the auto driver wander all over Cochin city, all because you did not know the correct address? You had no money left and had to wait the whole week for the royalty from your latest novel.

"If you had sent me a letter, arrangements could have been made for a guestroom for you," Achchan told you while paying the auto rickshaw driver.

"That was not possible, there wasn't enough time. Actually, I had other plans but something else cropped up. Maheshji and I were together till Bangalore. This is all because of my carelessness. I apologise for the inconvenience. Actually, it was only while I was passing through Kerala that I realized that I should stop here and attempt to understand the culture from within. And to do that I didn't want to stay in a guest house but within a Keralite household, therefore, Maheshji..."

"OK, OK, you did the right thing. It is our pleasure to offer you our hospitality. Let's talk inside in the sitting room. Maali, tell Amma to send some tea and snacks."

Toying with the curtain at the door, I was watching you with astonishment. Achchan reprimanded me again.

"...and listen Maali, with Raghu's help, clean Ranjan Ammaran's room upstairs."

"Why Ranjan Ammaran's room?"

"Do as you are told."

"Yes, Achchan."

You were eating upma, without relishing it. Deep inside I was laughing at your predicament. You were badly trapped, Mr Writer.

Ranjan Ammaran's room is a very special one. There are windows on either side. On one side it overlooks a huge compound filled with rubber, coffee and coconut trees. On the other – a view of the backwaters. Blue velvet curtains, old teak wood furniture. The trophies he had won, framed appreciation letters, rare artefacts: altogether a magical world which attracted me immensely in my childhood.

Those moments are strongly imprinted in my memory – when in a yellow and red pawada, sometimes in a green satin frock, two plaits tied with ribbons, a dot of kohl on my cheeks to keep away the evil eye, I used to secretly watch Ammaran – observe each action – smoking a cigarette while seated on the rocking chair lost in thought, reading. Truly, Ranjan Ammaran was a royal personality. Right now he stays in London. But whenever he returns, he occupies his own room. He would spend hours talking to Amma in this very room.

There was this longing in my heart to, once again today, open Mama's room and take out some volumes of English romantic poetry, nowadays rarely to be found even in Delhi's best bookstores.

I don't know whether you know or not that we Malayali Nayars follow the matrilineal system. This huge circular house with expensive teak wood doors, pillars and floor belongs to my mother and will be my inheritance. But who wants to stay here? I want to leave like Achchan, like you. To roam around. My mother has never left this small town and my father has lived here for a very little time. He always had one foot in Delhi, the other in Cochin. Achchan was very learned in both languages, Hindi and Malyalam, employed in the Bhartiya Sahitya Parishad. I inherited his love for Hindi.

Amma wasn't really happy with your coming...neither before nor after. Achchan kept explaining to Amma, later, "You don't understand. He is a great scholar and writer. Travelling all over this country and abroad. Writing is his profession. No one can become a great writer at such a young age without possessing any inborn talent. I have stayed in this same Maheshji's vacant flat without paying rent for two whole years – the one who wrote this letter."

"Isn't one writer enough that another one had to turn up? Writers! Their whole tribe is worthless." Grumbling, Amma headed towards the courtyard through the narrow passage guarding the free end of her sari from father's polluting touch. Achchan made a face as he glared at her. Then he said in Hindi, "I am an untouchable... Maali, if your mother touches me, she too will become an untouchable."

That evening I was startled when it rained heavily and you took the rocking chair out on to the balcony behind the room and sat there. You were smoking a cigarette, just like Ranjan Ammaran. And contemplating something within that self-created fog of smoke. I mistook you for Ranjan Ammaran. The only difference was your blue khadi kurta and white pyjamas. Ranjan Ammaran is a complete Englishman.

A sudden pang of longing pierced me. My entire adolescence had been consumed by my infatuation for Ranjan Ammaran. Don't know who – maybe Amma or Muttachi, my grandmother, had put it in my mind that I would get married to Ranjan Ammaran. Regardless of the objections of the outside world. In my inner world, Ranjan Ammaran was my first love and always will be.

There is no similarity between Ranjan Ammaran's appearance and yours. You are tall and fair. With light grey eyes. He is a dark complexioned man of medium height with beautiful eyes. There was a time when he too was quite romantic. The girls of the college in Kochi were crazy about him. One of them – a fair Syrian Christian girl even used to come home. But Ranjan Ammaran broke everyone's heart, including that of this fourteen-year-old niece of his, and married a foreign woman in London.

You were a little disturbed when you saw Ranjan Ammaran's room. "Nayar Sahib, I am not used to such magnificence. A small vacant room in a corner would be fine for me."

"Malayji, this room was supposed to witness the birth of a major English writer and philosopher but the process was cut short. World literature resides in these walls. This is my brother-in-law, Ranjan's room, who is a business tycoon in UK. The cupboards that you can see are stuffed with rare, world famous books. Please stay here. In a few days, you will begin to like it."

You had chosen a comparatively less crowded corner for your writing. You took a fancy to the room's huge teak study table. You made a makeshift settee for yourself next to it by spreading a cotton mattress. Whenever your legs tired of dangling at the table, you would place a desk on the floor and write on it. Except for those rainy nights when showers came through the window to soak the mattress.

In those early days, you never came down. Achchan would send up snacks, food and other things to you himself. Don't know which story you were writing. Awesome language is your gift. Believe me, I was becoming terribly excited.

After a few days, the responsibility of looking after you fell exclusively on my shoulders. Amma found you irritating. Muttachi had become old. In the morning, Raghu had to supervise the workers in our coffee, rubber and coconut plantations. Only Kinna would be cooking in the kitchen.

"Kinna is not a servant. She is a distantly related orphan and has stayed with me since childhood. Her marriage has been fixed too." I had told you once.

"'Hers too', does that mean yours as well?"

"Please!"

One morning, I saw you teaching Kinna how to make aaloo paranthas flouting Amma's puritanical rules.

Flustered, I asked, "Malayji, what is your caste?"

"If I say Muslim, then?"

"Stop it, you have a Hindu name."

"But why?"

"Only high caste people can enter Amma's kitchen, pure vegetarians, and that too after a bath and prayers."

You had smiled. Kinna too. So did I.

The first week you dejectedly partook of Keralite cuisine. Then, thanks to Kinna, you started getting aaloo paranthas and curd. In the afternoon, lunch was prepared totally under Amma's supervision, therefore you had to eat the rice sambhar and rasam. Breakfast was Kinna's and my joint responsibility. At that time, Amma would be busy offering prayers at various temples in the city. This was the only time I had with you. The only time you were not writing. The only time we could talk.

"What are you writing?"

"A long story."

"On love?"

"No."

"I have read your earlier stories. Achchan, who finds the word romance irritating, gave me your books to read. But what kind of romance do you portray? Absolutely terrifying, intense, harsh, a wasteland. Cathartic, deathly, pain-giving."

"Don't write all that now."

"Why?"

"That has all been spent. That word, love, does not create the same thrill anymore.

"That word 'love' has multiple meanings. There's a lot more to it than just thrills and sensation."

"No matter what implicit meanings may be in the word all its definitions are hollow. To write on it now would be mere repetition."

"Have you loved a lot?"

"Yes, everyone does, at the right age."

"Is there a special age to fall in love?"

"Isn't there? You are at that age."

I was taken aback at this unexpected answer. But the conversation was a thrill in itself. This conversation could be the source of inspiration, the beginning of a new story.

"Perhaps there should be other characters as well."

"There is. Your fiancé, Dr Sahib."

"So Achchan has told you. But can love of this sort exist? You write such enigmatic and complex emotional stories. You are not familiar with such ordinary human psychology."

"I know it, Vanja."

"Not Vanja, Vanmala."

"You're not Vanmala! You are Vanja, this jungle's creation."

You pointed towards the spreading rows of trees near the backwaters.

"So you have read all my stories. But, you haven't read the one in which unsuccessful love has been defined."

"I have read it."

" Then…"

"Then what? Your heart seems to be a graveyard."

"Really! How?"

You laughed uninhibitedly, emerging from the shell of your usually guarded laughter.

"Each story is the grave of a love."

In just a few moments, warmth had spilled over into the air from your laughter. One brackish chuckle remained. Like the wind that blows from the ocean.

In the days that followed, there was another such time too. Dusk was falling. We were on the small terrace from which beer-coloured waves could be seen rising. You had sniffed my freshly washed hair and asked, "Have you washed it with beer?"

I was reminded of one of the lines in your novel. 'On those special days of the month, girls are as fragrant as beer.'

I was stunned. You sensed my confusion in my telltale eyes and probed it. I abandoned my diffidence to disclose all to you.

You were silent for a long time, then smiled and said, "I write and forget, I suppose I must have written it."

"So all that has no meaning."

"Oh! When I'm writing, I write what comes to my mind – carried along by that spontaneous flow."

"Even episodes of love?"

"Yes, and what else?"

My heart broke. Those words in which I kept trying to trace the meaning of life with my wandering fingers, he writes and forgets. I was overcome with sadness. At first you studied my despondent face deeply, then grabbed my hair in your fist and smelt it again.

I asked you, "Should I leave?"

"No, keep talking."

"About what?"

"That graveyard. My heart…I think you were right when you said that my heart is a graveyard. Occasionally memories come and sweep it. There are…so many matters, innumerable regrets."

"You are so complex, so unusual."

"True. How can a child's life be normal, who was born in special circumstances to exceptional parents?"

You had made me sit very close to you. It seemed as if you were talking to yourself, gently moving on the rocking chair.

"Do you want to know? Then listen – my father was a Gandhian, a freedom fighter. My mother was his second wife, second illegal wife, who took the decision to live apart from my father till I was fifteen years old. I was always closer to my mother. His decision to leave us did affect me. Today at the age of forty, I can perhaps understand his decision but then I was only fifteen years old. The love between my father and mother was remarkable and limitless like them. Unconditional, free of expectations, but then I…"

"Then what?"

"Then, after Ma was gone, for a while I joined the crowd of my father's legal, joint family. Noticing my silence and distress, my father soon sent me to boarding school. After that, I never returned to him. I went off to Mumbai."

"Why didn't you get married?"

"What difference would that make?"

"You would have formed bonds, would have been happy."

"Who has been tied down and been happy?"

"It is not possible that you haven't loved at all! How would you have become a successful writer of unsuccessful love stories? Or is your mother and father's unfulfilled love story behind every contention of unrealised or illicit love?"

"Arre, you are talking like a psychiatrist. Neither are you a psychiatrist nor am I a patient seated on a couch with closed eyes mumbling a monologue, that we should search for explanations for the problems of the present in the tangled heap of yesterday's tribulations."

You laughed, got up from the rocking chair. Went and stood by the railing of the terrace, lighted a cigarette.

"One thing you said is true. The second, a half-truth.

Honestly speaking, I have been in and out of relationships with many women. But I have never blamed my family past for the failure of those relationships. My parents loved their independence as well as each other. In my view, theirs was a successful love marriage. My father went to jail as a freedom fighter. Ma returned to Tibet. This was the end of a great love story. I was a disastrous by-blow that dropped from a moment of this love story. All my love relationships were out of the ordinary. Every woman whom I was associated with was unusual, different from the others. The trajectory of every relationship was singular and unique. Even each break up was special."

"Then what did you gain from each?"

"If you ask me truthfully, none of my relationships were one-night stands. Each of them was serious and deep. The first occurred in the seventies. Times were changing. I was growing up with the songs of the Beatles. Birth control had come of age. Women's Lib was being talked about. That time itself was extraordinary. It was a time of transition. An unusually modern woman, a non-conformist in a sense, she was around seven years older than me. So frank and open, for that period. Had a good open relationship with her in which there was equal sharing in every way – individualistic space and liberty, depravity as well as imperfection. If betrayal, then faith and mutual freedom as well. It was a relationship without walls. Come and go as you please. But it didn't last long. She felt the need to get married. According to her, when our yet-to-be-born child would go to school, his young classmates would not be able to understand the philosophy of this relationship. They would tease him. I was not at all prepared to be a father at the age of nineteen. Just before parting she had made two lines in the sand as a symbol of our separation. She said that we would definitely meet in the end. We met before she left on that flight. She was an air-hostess. Hers was also a name on the list of those who died in the much talked about Kanishka tragedy. She was five months pregnant. Since then, she and her love have remained at the centre of my life, her memories too."

I was listening silently. You finished your cigarette, and then came and sat on the rocking chair.

"My second lover was a theatre artist. But she did not have the passion of an artist. She used to smoke strange smelling mint cigarettes and read Kafka. She was terribly insecure and wanted to clutch me to herself. I began to feel suffocated. Before I could leave her, she got into a relationship with a novice producer-director of advertisement films. She was a victim of mental depression. One day, just after the launch of my play *Mrityugandh*, she jumped from her flat and committed suicide. That play had an aging schizophrenic woman like her as the central character."

Now I started getting bored with his strange love stories. I wanted to change the topic. The smell of frankincense burning on a grave emanated from them. I didn't want to listen any more and open up more graves of his past loves.

"How do you manage your expenses? You don't even have a job."

"I manage to get by. Royalty from books, translations, the generosity of friends. By the way, my father put some money in the bank for me, in my name. Till now, I haven't felt the need for it. One flat...but so far, I haven't touched that money. The necessity didn't arise. Poor Tibetans sent by my mother live in the flat. I stay in that same old rented room. I'm used to it, the three cornered room… I am missing that room, Vanaja. Now, I'll leave soon."

Just a few days later, my new scooter arrived and I injured myself while learning to ride it. I was unable to raise my right hand as my elbow had a long and deep Chinese dragon-shaped bruise and my shoulder muscles were in shock due to the impact of the fall on the road.

You were working on that story with great seriousness. Shut up in your room. Battling your labour pains. But you came down at once when you heard about it from Raghu. You saw my room for the first time, examined it carefully. It was quite like Ranjan Ammaran's room, large and circular in shape, in the traditional Kerala style with a wooden floor and ceiling. A collection of old black and white ancestral pictures on the wall caught your attention. The pictures had been positioned so randomly that, now after you came to my room, that disarray seemed artful to me. At the moment you were looking at the huge antique Tanjore painting that hung behind the bed.

With the windows closed, there was little light in the room. Two brass lamps, wrought like horsemen, hung from hooks in the wooden ceiling. I was lying in a huge teak bed with a blue mosquito net surrounding it. You could not catch sight of me in the dim light. But I could see you clearly.

Achchan called out, "Vanmala."

I pretended to be startled and sat up.

Achchan removed the mosquito net. My washed-out face was revitalized, the way it always is the moment I see you.

"It wasn't a fracture?"

I shook my head. I was examining your face carefully. Had a week's seclusion and rest made you look younger?

"It will take four-five days to get better."

There were a few thick books in your hands.

"Sometimes it is good to be sick. You get time to ponder over life, to read what others have written. Sometimes I wish to be sick for a long time. Read these."

You looked into my eyes and smiled faintly. I was surprised and asked myself, what kind of sick call was this?

I was oscillating between the extremes of severe pain and the ensuing relief medication provided. Completely disoriented by the shock of the injury. Alongside, a light bluish shadow of lust was taking shape – between the flickering yellow flames of high fever and pain. In such a situation to read the love passage between the Naxalite hero and journalist heroine in your recently published revolutionary novel! Word by word, it was awakening a dream within me. A longing for your tranquil, cool palms arose. A longing for hands that would halt the progress of my fever – soothe my pain, absorb my heat.

For the first time, it felt romantic to be sick. My emotional upheaval had been blunted by the searing pain, the soaring fever. A vision took birth, a vision of the flesh. I took out all your books and searched through them for steamy love passages and read them over and over again.

Chhee! How brazen you become in some places. Ouf! I became so aroused that I lost sense of any limits. I don't know how, afterwards, still burning with fever, I found myself outside your room. You were awake. The acrid smell of cigarette smoke was filtering in through the window. Maybe you were sitting next to the window and had seen my shivering shadow.

Confused, you hurried out.

"Why are you here, at this time?"

"I don't know."

"Oh!"

"Show me the story.

"Which one?"

"The one that you are writing about me."

"I'm not writing it now. But yes, I will write it. About you. Once there was Vanaja who had big black eyes. There was Suresh."

You were trying to distract me, stave off the obstinacy awakened by my fever and my desire.

"No, the one that you are writing right now."

"You are not in that one."

"I know I am there. Otherwise, why did you smell my hair that day."

A copper coloured moon had appeared. Moonlight dripped from it like molten copper upon the frothy fringe formed by the waves in the ocean.

"Go downstairs."

"No."

Determinedly, I went inside and picked up the scored through, incomplete draft from the desk. You snatched the papers from my hand roughly and pushed me on the bed.

"You are not in this story and there is nothing romantic, you fool."

My ardour made me forget myself. I remembered Ranjan Ammaran kissing his lover passionately in this very bed. In the month of chaith, a field of wheat was maturing on my flesh. You could have gone through it. I wanted it. You should have gathered the scattered golden sand of my trembling flesh.

You did nothing of the sort. Just sat on your rocking chair and puffed away at your cigarette angrily. I was babbling like someone overcome by a hysterical fit. You had no sympathy for me. I don't know when Achchan came and stood there. His eyes went wide with shock and outrage. I was frightened. You were not scared, kept smoking your cigarette. You did not offer any clarifications. Achchan dragged me away. The wound in my elbow struck against the door and opened up again. Blood began to drip from it.

A storm did blow up. But was contained within the bounds of a respectable family's reputation. Suppressed, covered up. What came to you was just a harsh request. Despite all my clarifications on your behalf, my arguments. "Malayji, the date of Vanmala's wedding has been fixed. The house will soon be full of guests. So that you are not inconvenienced, I will make arrangements for you elsewhere or make a reservation for Delhi if you have finished your writing."

Your face turned red with the insult, then acquired a purple and blackish hue. Even then, you did not utter a word in your defence.

"It would be better to return."

As I turn the pages of my diary, I find some days and a few memories hidden in it.

What kind of days are these? If I strain my memory, maybe I can capture their essence – cold or hot? Days like dismembered branches! Desiccated brown leaves were scattered on the roads. The weather, poised on the brink of change, was writing poems on the amaltas. The city had turned yellow with the rising humidity, baffled falling leaves and the amaltas trees! Surely, some fragrance of that time will linger in my memories...

You are reflective again today. There is pain, but not that of creativity in these ruminations. My heart is plummeting. Kinna quietly observes my agony and then looks at you. I am infatuated, besotted by the words written by you...by your voice. I am obsessed with the softness, the sweetness hidden within your coarse and hard persona. You are sitting sad and lonely besides the speeding current of your years. I await your return to life.

Tomorrow you will leave. Your meagre luggage, all packed, is informing me. You have collected everything: the vast expanse of your incongruity, your scattered self as well. I found three toothpicks strewn in the garden at the back. I have saved them with care. As I move forward, a heap of torn pages. Oh! This is the same story that you had begun before me.

Again, you set out at night even though your train was at eight in the morning. Wandering aimlessly through the web of narrow lanes to the same cheap bar run by that notorious Vellu! You will return in the middle of the night.

One shoe fell off the bed with a thump. You have returned. It is one o' clock. I remain awake till five in the morning.

Maybe you had remembered the rules of courtesy and thoughtfully put down the second shoe gently.

You were badly trapped, Mr Writer. Muttering to myself, I began to sob. Dozed off exhausted at five in the morning. A dreamy voice awakens my consciousness. A voice that says little. A voice with few words – a captivating voice. Like a necklace with just a few pearls, a rushing river containing very few rocks. This voice has been deceiving my heart. As far as love is concerned, I am convinced that there is nothing like it any more!

"Anything new?" When I return from college and enter your room.

And today a voice emerged from your shadow as it turned to smoke in the mist of dawn.

"I am leaving, Vanaja."

At this point, I feel that if this voice did not remain, the magnitude of this vast world would turn into nothingness, as if, this enthralling voice was building a bridge between heaven and earth. My heart wanted to scream and say, "I touched your story. So what? Why did you discard it, not just rejected it but pushed it away like a bird rolling away her wasted nest. Am I an untouchable? Look, I still have the broken shells of that story. Oh! How callously you have ripped the draft apart. It is impossible to piece it together." For a long time, I kept trying to join the fragments of that story together like a jigsaw puzzle at the dining table.

I was searching for myself. You were right when you said that I was not anywhere in the story. I really am nowhere. There is an old astrologer with a tame parrot that picks up the fortune cards with its beak, an old building with many wings where tenants live fighting amongst themselves. An intoxicated nomad who lives with the memory of that old man. A woman like a waterfall.

Where am I? There is nothing romantic in this.

*Translated by Prem K. Srivastava and Gitanjali Chawla*

# Utopia

Vandana Rag

Najjo did not have a father.

He had passed away when she was barely two. Najjo couldn't remember what he had looked like. She had once seen a faded black and white picture in Ammi's trunk, the one with pink flowers and green leaves on its lid. While playing, she had run into the dark, suffocating little room at the rear end of the house. It was pitch dark. You couldn't see anything there, but the inexplicable allure of the petal and leaf-strewn lid of the trunk drew Najjo on. Tripping and tumbling, she reached the trunk and climbed on it. There she stood, preening, daintily clutching the edges of her frock and swaying from left to right. It suddenly struck her that all her acrobatics had failed to set the trunk clanging... why? She plonked herself down cross-legged in front of it, and proceeded to wrestle with the lid. Her little palms found the latch and her eyes lit up. She clasped it tightly, tugged hard and the lid sprang open. Wah! Inside was lots of interesting stuff, shimmering and glittering. She saw a pearl studded purse, a hand fan with a blue chenille frill, lots of silverware, which had a dingy grey appearance, and beneath, much beneath all these things, lay buried a gharara suit with a somewhat blackened sheen. Najjo's eyes gleamed even more.

"Ya Allah! A wedding dress!" She had seen several such dresses at those innumerable weddings she had attended, holding Ammi's finger, clinging to her, inseparable as her shadow. This quirk would often invite much bantering. "Najjo, let go of your mother's finger. Will you take her away as part of your dowry? Let go!" Little Najjo's eyes would tingle with tears, but her spirited obduracy would blaze through them: "I'll never leave my Ammi and go anywhere."

"Oh yes?" the women would retort, rolling their eyes and twirling their hands. "You won't get married?"

"No!" she'd cloak her obstinacy in an angry scream. "I'll never get married."

The women would laugh heartily and Ammi would immediately turn her palms over her little head to ward off the evil eye, saying, "May Allah have mercy! That's not to be said, child!"

But this early stubbornness lingered to become part of her personality and continued to resonate firmly in her heart. Her family came to understand this much later in retrospect… Najjo, however, knew everything. It was all her game. She had planned it.

Najjo pulled out the dress and turned it over and over

untidily. The very idea of marriage repulsed her, and yet the wedding dress warmed her heart with an incomprehensible joy. She wanted to dress up in the red outfit and prance around and show off, and yet never leave her Ammi's side. Her inordinate attachment to Ammi often worried her brothers. "Ammi, agreed she's the only daughter. Agreed, she's the youngest. Agreed that Abbu is no more, but this excessive attachment does not seem right. And you, too, let her get away with a lot. She's turning more and more stubborn day by day." Ammi would stop ladling the saalan for just a moment. She'd turn around to size up her three sons and her heart would warm to them.

The pain of her husband's loss would be half reduced. All her three sons had grown into sensible young men. Her beloved Pappu, Guddu and Raja. His father's employers had taken Pappu on, as a driver after the latter's demise. He had then managed to get similar jobs for both his brothers, using his contacts. Together, the three brothers managed to raise an income of ten to twelve thousand rupees a month. As of now, all was well. But Ammi knew that everything would have to be reworked once their brides arrived. Najjo's marriage too would have to be arranged in another four or five years. She was the darling of her heart, but she couldn't really hug her to her breast forever. She was pampered no end. Perhaps that had made her a little self-willed. But Ammi didn't make much of it. She knew that by the time girls are nudging twelve or thirteen, they begin to mind themselves with great alacrity. Good sense slices right through their frolics and tantrums, and takes complete charge. Then they don't even need to be told to take care of their dupattas.

The slightest hint of a slip and they become alert and watch out for themselves. Ammi too, had grown up traversing the same route. Had learnt to keep her dupatta in place, abide by the strictures of the namaz along with acquiring efficiency in cooking saalan. So while she understood her sons' concern, she didn't give it too much importance. What was to be done? Girls will grow unrestrained like the shoots of a wild shrub, and they must. It was a matter of just a few more years. Then where would Najjo prattle about their house? She'd have to go and thrive elsewhere, under someone else's protection. Completely within it. Ammi often worried herself sick over this. Her husband had never insisted on the veil: she did not have to don a burkha, was merely expected to cover herself with a chador. But who knew what Najjo's in-laws would be like?

Ammi's eyes would smile benignly at her sons, reassuring them. She was there for all of them. The boys respected Ammi. They were employed, they worked sincerely, they stayed away from unnecessary quarrels and arguments.

Stirring her saalan, suddenly Ammi thought of her daughter, who had been missing for a while. Missing daughters inevitably rendered homes traumatized and forlorn, Ammi knew. This little bird flitting about her home added exquisite meaning to her existence. She felt lonely without her incessant chatter. But where was she? Brushing away the cobwebs that had sprung up on their own, Ammi called out, "Najjo... Najjo! Najjo!"

Najjo hadn't even examined the gharara suit properly when she dimly registered her mother's voice calling her from far as if echoing from a mountain to the plain beneath it. Not that Najjo had seen any valleys or mountains. She hadn't even seen villages or fields properly. Not even mapped the contours of this very town with her eyes for that matter. For her, this half plastered, half brick-lined house, a little away from the Rajiv Nagar locality, was effectively the whole world. Sometimes she'd set out on a jaunt to town, when any of her brothers finished their duty and still had the car with them. They gladly obliged her with these joyrides as often as they could. That apart, clinging to her Ammi's hand, she'd go visiting neighbours and relatives and that was it.

Ammi's echoing call terrified her no end, goodness knows why. Startled, she dropped the gharara suit. When it fell to the floor she heard a crackling sound and with it came the magical patter of Ammi's steps. "Arre, Najjo, what are you doing here in the dark...? What have you smashed...? Illillah! What shenanigans will this girl come up with next...? Where the hell are you...?" For the first time in her life Najjo heard her Ammi rage like other mothers. For the first time she encountered the stinging, sharp edge of her mother's palm instead of its usual rabbity softness.

For the first time she learnt that in smashing that buried article, she had damaged the one precious thing her mother had secretly treasured for so many years. That day, for the first time, a sad melody stirred in her little heart. That sorrow wrenches the heart and streams out through the eyes – Najjo learnt this too, that very day. Despite the calamitous magnitude of her distress she had somehow gleaned that Ammi's rage was justified. When she was pulled out of the dark room and flung into the light, she understood that even light could hurt the eyes when they are suddenly forced open after darkness. It feels as if nails are being hammered into them. In between this painful dose of knowledge Ammi informed her, while showing her the photograph with its shattered glass and fractured frame over and over again, how she had thoughtlessly smashed the only photograph of her father. That day, she had learnt how dark her Abbu had been. Dark with a long, brown beard. In the midst of her newly earned tribulations she had found a sliver of happiness. She wasn't like Abbu at all; she was like her Ammi, fair and beautiful. Tearfully, she extricated Abbu's picture from Ammi's limp hands. Now she was in Ammi's lap wrapping Ammi's arms around herself, removing her from the vanished past to the present and lending them a sense of purpose yet again.

"You crazy thing!" Was Ammi speaking, or just sobbing? "There was just one picture of your Abbu, and now it'll have to be framed again."

"Ammi," began Najjo, pushing everything away with the frank curiosity of her years, "why do you keep Abbu's picture locked in the trunk? It could've been hung up here with these," she pointed to the bright pictures of Mecca and Medina embossed on black fabric. "I am sure they wouldn't mind, and we could've seen Abbu everyday, even though he wasn't around."

"No..." Ammi's gloom was dense. Najjo couldn't reach through it. She was too young.

"Why not, Ammi?" she persisted; her impetuousness getting the better of her distress. Ammi was thrown off balance. How could she make this little mite understand?

She had a firm belief she'd learn on her own. Being a girl – the right demeanour, the boundaries of her life, roza, namaz and whatever else, would be learnt soon enough.

She tenderly hoisted Najjo from her lap, stood her on the floor and tried pulling the edge of her frock below her knees – in vain. It couldn't be pulled any further. The girl had shot up. Soon it would have to be salwar kameez. Her legs were growing so long and smooth, and, inshallah, she had a gloriously bright wheatish complexion. She had big, black eyes, and her hair was long and black. Her plait kept bouncing on her back. The sooty outlines of her eyes snaked out to sting. No wonder her younger sister-in-law had declared, "Baaji, Najjo will come into our family only. The men of this family look completely unimpressive, as it is. This girl will bring cheer to our eyes. And hopefully improve the line." Ammi had long sensed the earnestness masked in this casual repartee. The prospect terrified her. Wouldn't her darling be suffocated with such a stern mother-in-law? She would say "yes", and inwardly summon all her prayers that it may never be so. She had even told her sons once that Najjo would be best settled outside the family. Her sons had stopped giving importance to such utterings. They knew that when it came to Najjo, Ammi and Ammi alone would decide everything; no matter what they said.

The next afternoon Ammi slipped out, leaving Najjo playing at home, braving the blistering heat for an all-important purpose. She had a running account at Agarwal and Sons. The seth saw her and brightened with joy as he would at the sight of such customers. In this small town, his trade thrived thanks to those customers, who unable to pay cash down, were perpetually in his debt. This way their number never decreased, even if it meant that he couldn't recover his costs immediately. He was content in the assurance that they could never desert him. This was a classic case of deferred returns, which would yield dividends in the future. The seth did not worry too much about his debtors. Where could they possibly disappear to? Eventually they'd pay up, and if not, well, there was the police and the party workers ever ready to assist him. After all, he paid hefty taxes to both, being one who was numbered amongst the big businessmen of the town.

"Tell me, what would you like to see?" he infused a syrupy sweetness into his voice. Ammi regarded the seth as acceptably decent, even though somewhere she sensed he wasn't. Despite her many debts, his syrupy sweetness had remained more or less consistent. The embarrassment of being in debt can be killing enough, without the shopkeeper's rudeness to add to your woes. Moreover, as of now Ammi had to fend for her brood, so she had to maintain her relationship with this expensive but sweet syrup. She put her hand on a roll of cotton fabric with a beige base, printed with little red flowers.

"Bhaiya, three metres of this and a red georgette dupatta to match the flowers."

"Dupatta would be…?"

"A meter and a half."

The seth looked into Ammi's eyes and thickening the syrup said, "Oh! You're shopping for bitiya? Then why this cotton? There's this Benarsi stuff that has come in. Take some of that. The wedding season is also round the corner. She'll dazzle in this. Ay, boy! Show her the Benarsi fabric." His sweetness transformed into the severity of a broom's harsh stroke. Ammi didn't mind. He had maintained her status – above that of his servant. The boy dumped the roll of cloth down with a hint of defiance. Ammi sensed it and bolstered by the strength of the syrup said, "Arre bhaiya, show it properly." The twice-battered servant sat with his legs folded and got on with his job with thorough professionalism. The lesson to keep his emotions out of his work was something that had been administered to him in childhood like an essential tonic.

"Here, take a look. Which one?" Ammi's eyes opened wide. What gorgeous fabric, what lovely colours! All brocaded in gold. As if golden flowers were growing out of the fabric itself. She liked the yellow one best of all. She felt these golden flowers on turmeric yellow would suit her darling's glorious wheatish complexion and she'd blossom like a thousand blooms. Yearning, she asked, "But this would be expensive?"

"Not at all… It is Benarasi, but at half the price." The seth shored Ammi up by adding, "Benarasis now make cloth for folks like us too." Ammi ordered three meters of the fabric and shelled out two hundred rupees from her worn old purse. "Get the dupatta matched and add the remaining amount to next month's account." The seth swooped on the money, wrote three hundred in the remainder column, and in his usual post transaction gesture, fixed his gaze on the drawers of his table.

Ammi too, picked up her purchase, stuffed in blue

polythene, and left the shop. She thought she'd stitch the cotton suit herself, but get the seamstress Shakeela to do the Benarasi one. She stitched excellent ladies' suits. She had recently made one for herself. Thinking about her suit, Ammi was overcome by a strange embarrassment. She sucked in her breath. She had never worn anything but a sari all these years, but some time back her eldest son, referring to some conversation after the namaz in the mosque had said, "Ammi, Maulvi sahib was saying that women will have to wear salwar kameez at namaz. Saris are too revealing." Hearing her son talk like that at her age, she shuddered. At fifty-five, even if a bit of her stomach was visible, what was there to see? Half revealed stretch marks and loose, hanging skin? Did that qualify for nakedness if anyone's eye fell on it? It was simply the result of bearing many children. Most of the neighbourhood women had respected the maulvi's injunctions and taken to wearing salwar kurtas. Something like a fledgling anger would rise within Ammi. She feared she'd be made an outcaste for not heeding the maulvi's call. What if somebody said something offensive to her...? As a result, hesitantly, she began wearing salwar suits for the namaz.

Shakeela had a hearty laugh when she saw the cloth. "Why, Najjo's Amma, have proposals already begun to pour in for your daughter?"

"No, no..." Ammi supported Shakeela's enthusiasm with a smile.

"Arre, your daughter is like the moon, cover her up as much as you will, she'll glow all the same. You'll have to guard her carefully. There's a growing army of lads in the locality.

And these Hindu boys have become too overbearing. As it is, things are not too good. And for a girl – how does Hindu or Muslim matter?"

All this filled Ammi with an unknown trepidation. "She's only in the fifth standard as of now. When she is in the eighth, I'll get her engaged," she decided, and only after forcing Shakeela to reduce her charges did she leave her shop.

The heat beat down oppressively. Ammi felt she would melt away by the time she got home. She pulled her pallu over her head and quickened her pace. Her steps made her light blue sari swish in the breeze. Ammi just couldn't figure out when she ran into Maulvi Usman Ali. He stopped short on seeing her and after saying, "Salaam Valekkum," stopped her for a little chitchat. Ammi's eyes turned wary. She glanced past him to check out the visible folds of her stomach, tried to figure out if any nakedness was apparent. Maulvi Sahab meanwhile was proclaiming in his sharp tone, after ejecting a spray of paan: "The times are bad, Bibi, the young ones, the boys, will have to be given guidance. It's all because of this TV and cinema…! Now, how many sermons can I give? When the family elders don't understand, what can we possibly expect to tell children? Young men have stopped coming to the mosque for namaz. Now they turn up only on Fridays. This isn't right." The Maulvi stroked his long brown beard with an air of dejection. Something seethed in Ammi's breast. She found this discourse utterly unendurable.

She whispered, "Yes, yes." and tried to get away. And lo and behold! Maulvi Usman stepped aside and began to walk along with her. Trying to make the best of the situation, Ammi said, "My sons, Maulvi sahib, try to abide by the namaz, whenever they are not on duty, wherever they may be."

"I didn't mean your sons. I was talking of the world in general. Bibi, money! Big money is being squandered by all the well-heeled seths on Hindu festivals. Now look at this. They have the gall to set up their Nav Durga Samiti right next to the mosque. All this is to harass us. There's an army of goons, who go around singing and drumming, creating a ruckus to disrupt our namaz."

"Oh yes, " Ammi replied to cut him short.

But the Maulvi was in no mood to stop, he railed on, "This time that young fellow has become in charge of the Samiti. The good-for-nothing!"

"Who?" Ammi inquired. "Arre, the same one – from your locality. The one whose father used to set up a fruit stall at Farookh Mian's shop. What a decent man he was! Farookh and he got along so well. And look at the son? Has never done a stroke of work, but is getting up to all this. They spoil the atmosphere, Bibi."

Ammi's furtive eyes now sought her heart. The boy Maulvi sahib was talking about was someone she had found very sweet till a few years back. Najjo's father had had a good equation with his father, and they'd often visit each other's homes. These were all tales of bygone times. Now it wasn't possible. Ammi let out an embarrassed sigh. It seemed as if the entire social fabric of this town had altered. She had indeed coddled and pampered that boy much as a child. He had such lovely pink lips, as beautiful as a girl's. Yes, she didn't quite like his name, a lengthy tongue twister of sorts. Achyutanand Gosain. He would play in the vacant plot adjacent to her house with other children of the locality. They would often gang up and come to their house seeking funds for the Durga festival. During the last two years, this fund raising expedition had petered out. Earlier, when they came asking for money, it felt like a nuisance to Ammi, but the disruption in this practice, so many years old, registered harsh and loud. Its venom often erupted afresh, like pain in a festering wound, pointing to a change that Ammi was not prepared to acknowledge readily. This town was so unlike the town of her childhood years. The Muslims today were, of course, different from what they had been in those times. Education, employment, in everything the graph was going up, but there was also this inexplicable failure to understand each other, this hardening to the very core. This hardening impacted just about everything around. It was within the Muslims and without, within the Hindus too. Ammi's sons would carry news of the whole world. They used to take out big 'parties' for tours to Agra, Delhi or Mysore. She would hear about those places and see them all, from the Lal Quila to the Taj Mahal. She even began to understand leaders and politics a little, thanks to her sons, the newspapers and TV. She knew very little, but understood a great deal. "Be careful" was becoming the philosophy of her existence. When, almost imperceptibly, people's faces were changing and the warmth of relationships that had existed for years began to melt and flow away, then one just had to seek cover, take hold of one's feelings and withdraw into a shell; into grimy pigeonholes – like singed rams crammed in their stalls. Afraid, but carrying on the business of living, fortified by false hopes, the belief in the security of sticking together. Who knew who might be stationed outside the pen, on the lookout for fresh meat? Maulvi Usman Ali's discourse, though unacceptable, did toll the alarm bells of truth. She felt like shooing off the wretch to some place else, he only aggravated the confusions she was trying to fend off. She began to say, "Khuda Hafiz," but cut it short just in time. She was used to this greeting ever since she was a child, but of late was using 'Allah Hafiz' – more at the behest of her sons. 'Allah' insisted on a substantial acknowledgement of His existence. People in the community now preferred the weight and verbosity of 'Allah' to the pleasant lightness of 'Khuda'. As a result, 'Allah Hafiz' too had become a part of her being like salwar kameez. She mustered all the composure she could and said, "Allah Hafiz." Maulvi Usman Ali did not like being short changed like this. He began to complain, "Ay, won't you even offer me a cup of tea?"

"Oh!" Ammi's objection was effective. "I have to go to the market, there are no vegetables at home."

"All right," the Maulvi replied, clearly airing his disappointment, but Ammi just would not take the hint. She turned him away from the very door of her house and hastened inside.

The outer room was cemented and plastered and adjacent to this was Pappu's room. Ammi thought she'd get at least three rooms plastered by and by. For the brides of her three sons. Najjo, inshallah, would leave for her husband's home. As far as she was concerned, it didn't matter. A bed could be laid in the outer room for her. Allah be thanked, the desperate circumstances they had fallen into following the untimely demise of Najjo's father, were improving steadily.

"Najjo... Najjo!" she called out. Najjo appeared, pulling the red dupatta Ammi had brought over her head and began posing coquettishly. Ammi immediately turned her palms over her head, and pressed her knuckles to her own temples, warding off the evil eye. Najjo's blooming paved the way to imminent dangers. She decided that she'd stitch loose, baggy kurtas for her daughter and instruct Shakeela to do the same.

A gang of lads from the locality used to create a ruckus on the empty plot next to Najjo's house, which they used as a playground. Lately, Ammi had prohibited Najjo from going and playing with them, because every evening she would come home looking harassed. Earlier, she used to be a regular participant in the cricket games played there. The boys would make her field and laugh at her clumsy, awkward gait as she struggled to keep up with them.

There, once Atchyutanand Gosain had hit numerous shots and made her chase the ball endlessly. The boys doubled up with laughter at her plight, and Najjo, finally unable to bear her exhaustion and humiliation, sat in a heap and buried her sobbing head between her knees. When she raised her head again, Atchyutanand Gosain had his first encounter with two burning pomegranates framed by hissing snakes. For a moment he was frightened and began to descend into an incomprehensible dejection. For some reason, he felt like crying. He wanted to pluck out those pomegranates from her cheeks and fling them away. Why were they so red? He wanted to pierce her eyes. Why were they so black? Why were they hurting him? He closed his eyes, and when his friends finally nudged him to open them, Najjo had disappeared from the scene. He felt as if the landscape before his eyes had gone absolutely blank, like a gaping chasm of terror that could never be filled up. Najjo never came back to occupy that empty space and its emptiness took possession of Atchyutanand's heart like a threat that would never go away.

A year passed in growing up. Atchyutanand acquired a downy moustache. His voice cracked and turned hoarse. His clothes became smaller and he stopped playing cricket on the plot next to Najjo's house. The boy was beset with two simultaneous misfortunes. His father's untimely death forced him to abandon his carefree freedom and sit at the fruit-seller's shop; and the incessantly growing blank space in his heart made him increasingly restless. Thus afflicted, his mind descended steadily into a hazy chaos.

One day, he was sitting in the shop, overcome with boredom, when Councillor Sri Ram Mohan appeared and told his brother, "Why have you tied up the boy in this business? Let him join us. We'll train him in the party's work. Settling your accounts at this age, he'll turn grey in the first flush of youth."

The elder brother had no talent beyond his trade. Overwhelmed, he folded his hands and replied, "Take him sir, turn him into a proper man. I'll hire someone to help me. Please take him under your wing."

Councillor Sri Ram Mohan began to laugh, "Come, get up and come with me right away. Hold this bag of fruit..." Papayas and cheekoos were nursing each other's bruises inside the bag. Atchyutanand was furious with himself. Why did he see people imaged in fruits, and fruits imaged in people all the time? At times he felt like chopping people up like fruit. First bite them with his teeth and then, if they proved too stubborn and inflexible, slice them through with a sharp knife. He experienced everything as struggling inside a fog in his mind. This haze had deepened with his father's death. He had been expelled from school after flunking thrice in a row. Even otherwise, how long could a seventeen-year-old continue to study in the seventh standard? He enjoyed playing the role of the local tough for a year or two, but eventually even that got boring. Atchyutanand was looking for viable alternatives and goals when Sri Ram Mohan incarnated in his life. He didn't like him very much. Fat, podgy, with cheeks like watermelons. He was often tempted to put a knife to them to see if they were really red inside. But he was a useful man. He knew how to grow money, to provide a living to unemployed young men like him. In return, he also knew how to get much work out of them. And by assembling them together in a group and encouraging them to pursue certain activities, provided them with a sense of purpose beyond the immediate.

Initiation would begin with an excellent meal. Then the boys would be made familiar with the etiquette of drinking, beginning with beer. When they got into the habit of visiting his den, their coaching would begin. They would be made to listen to inspiring discourses on Indian culture and religion. Cadres would be trained to organize yajnas in town, and as members of the Festival Organization Committee they would take care of the celebrations of Hindu festivals. The boys would thus acquire an objective, and become devoted fans of Sri Ram Mohan. During the last two years, in the final phase of coaching for recruits, videotapes of various sadhus' speeches were being distributed throughout town for spiritual cleansing. It was hoped that caught young, these lads would imbibe the lessons properly and aid in the transformation of the atmosphere of the town.

The first assignment for Atchyutanand Gosain was to organize a yajna for Pakistan's defeat in an India-Pakistan cricket match. An auto rickshaw with a loudspeaker went blaring around the town. Banners were put up at important places in the market place and at the station. The whole town was soon abuzz. All the inhabitants were requested to affirm their faith in the nation. All the young party cadres were summoned. Many people turned up and all sat down to pray for India's success. Along with the live telecast, people watched Atchyutanand Gosain's face flush crimson in the midst of chants of, "Om Swaha...Om Swaha..." His face glowed with the radiance of his passionate devotion to the nation. His chest expanded, so much so, that he began to cough fitfully. People rushed to him with water. When, later, India defeated Pakistan by five wickets, his supporters hoisted him on their shoulders and carried him through the town. Cadres got into an open jeep and danced some sort of a balle balle bhangra to mark their celebrations. Atchyutanand was gaining the stature of a hero, as the townsfolk watched silently.

In the house next to the vacant plot in Rajiv Nagar colony too, everyone watched this on TV. The brat, who had made a girl from this house chase after a ball, was no longer an amateur cricketer of the locality. He had turned into a young man who worried more about the nation than a cricket ball. After watching the news, the rotis cooked in that house were baked on fires consumed with restlessness and suffocation. They tasted of smoke. Najjo wanted to spit out that taste in the bathroom and rinse it out with water. A spark of rage began to crackle within her. Nothing should be ruined by that ashen taste. Neither beds, nor chairs, nor doors, nor walls nor bathroom. The hearths should be washed afresh and the doors tightly shut to wall out those victory songs wafting in from the road. They belonged to the street. They were unworthy of being brought in. A kind of poison added intoxication to those songs and Najjo, for the first time since she began to grow up, articulated a dogged resolve the logic of which was lost on Ammi, despite her years and intelligence. "Ammi, put heavy curtains on these windows. There's just too much light and heat and dust. Especially on the windows facing the vacant plot. A searing loo blows in from there!"

Atchyutanand was being honed well. He was achieving an inner enlightenment but it battled with all sorts of impediments. It was full of different kinds of fruit, people in fruits and fruits in people. There were undefined gashes of memory, which cast dark shadows. This was a battle between illumination and fog, from which Sri Ram Mohan's training programme held out a strong promise of deliverance. His first encounter with this enlightenment came when he watched a video recording. He was dumbfounded. His arms and legs turned chill, freezing him into a heap. Somewhere, an old mosque. In some town called Ayodhya. In some corner of India. The video said that the mosque was built on false foundations. As the commentary continued, the mosque was being pulled down. "They ruled us thinking that we were lowly cowards, they ruled us… At least get together now and destroy this mosque, or be branded impotent. You need to give out the message that our race is not impotent, and those people need to understand that if they have to live here, they have to be loyal to this land."

The moment Atchyutanand heard the bit about them being loyal to this land, his temples began to throb. The glowing crimson pomegranates he had glimpsed some years ago kept flashing in his eyes. His mind kept reverting to the vacant plot and the inhabitants of the adjacent house. What was the connection between the video recording and the people of that house…? Be still! He let his taut frame relax and stepped out of Ram Mohan's den. Outside, the translucence of the evening was about to spread its wings. A rainbow hue slowly stretched across the sky. He turned into a kite strung between the sky and the road. He flew on, measuring the street, first the market place, then the station, then, with an inexplicable excitement, Rajiv Nagar and beyond it — the empty plot. He sat opposite it and noticed that the gulmohar tree at the end of the plot had grown swiftly and was blossoming with red flowers. This was a new development, since his departure from this place a few years ago. The sight of the young tree's red blossoms brought a thrill. He rose and tore off several bunches of flowers and placed them in that empty space, filling it up. The same blank spot that still bound him to this place;

which was the reason for the endless, gaping vacuum within him. Placing the flowers before him, he sat in the dust and closed his eyes, soaking in a rare delight – with the impossible thought that some part of his past might return to him right here. But only dark and ghastly images greeted his eyes, which possessed the terrifying face of some Babur and a clumsily demolished mosque. There were thousands of bricks, fresh from the kiln with the ineradicable name of Maryada Purushottam Ram engraved on them. And along with all this, legions of people who were carrying these bricks on their heads. In the midst of all that screaming and clamouring, just one sentence stood out with the strength of the assault of the multitudes, "Give it one more push."

Atchyutanand Gosain was overwhelmed with rage. For the past three years, the haze that Sri Ram Mohan, Councillor, had been trying to brighten had only grown denser. The evening had turned into night. It was getting dark, but the darkness spreading within was much greater. Atchyutanand groped for his eyes. He forced them open with a great effort and saw an almost invisible circle, the solid void trapped within him that he had tried to fill up with gulmohar blossoms. But no miracle occurred, nothing brought him joy. He got up abruptly. The dismembered flowers were withering fast. He trampled them with all the strength of his booted feet, kicked at the vacant spot and making a cloud of dust fly into the hazy dark, departed.

Ammi was right. There was no way to halt Najjo's blooming. Neither Ammi's loose fitting kurtas, nor the folds of her drapes, nor the rozas, nor the regimen of namaz, nor the safe confines of home and hearth. Beyond the locality and outside Najjo's Urdu School campus, long lines of admirers sprang up to catch her attention. But Najjo had become wise, exceedingly wise. She was totally devoted to her roza and namaz. Her conduct was often cited in Muslim households, and she felt safe in such homes. She felt that despite the thousand desires raging in her breast, she was better off as an Allah-fearing Muslim. She prayed that she'd never stray from the correct path. She was no longer the kid prancing around with her frock edges picked up. Now she wrapped her clothes around her properly and covered her face and head with her dupatta when she went out.

Meanwhile, her friends had a good time. The wooers suffered new pangs whenever they set their eyes on her. Almost every day they would find this particular Majnu, pushing back his hair, serenading away: *"Jhalak dikhla ja, ek bar aja aja aja..."* (Just show your face once, just come to me once) Her friends would laugh their guts out, teasing Najjo all the way, exuding a heady and pleasant fragrance in the breeze. Growing up definitely seemed like a lot of fun.

One day, the girls decided that after coming home from school, they'd change their clothes and go to the market. This time the Nav Durga Samiti had put a fabulous idol on display next to the mosque on the hillock. The idol was decked up in a dazzling dress and jewellery, and alongside there were some exhibits of religious scenes with moving electric lights. The girls set out, properly decked up. They glittered themselves, brightening the market place.

The dense crowds were being marshalled into neat rows to witness the decorations and the pageantry. The girls got into the queue and giggled their way forward. "Come on, move on please, don't crowd here," the volunteers issued instructions and people kept walking on. In the midst of all these voices, a deep, empty one was heard, "Please hand out the prasad, bhai!" Najjo's ears too registered the fragmenting syllables of that voice. She was irked by both – the vacancy and the heaviness. She raised her head to take a look. It was wrapped in her dupatta; only her face was visible while her frame was locked away in the folds of her dress. The people around her caught a glimpse and realized that she was a very young girl, merely trying to look older. The heavy but vacant voice, which seemed to be that of an old acquaintance, proved to belong to Atchyutanand Gosain. He became apparent first as a voice that eventually turned out to belong to a body. He too, looked up and his heart leapt, recognizing the object of an old quest. Amidst the dense crowd, his vision was absolutely clear: and he only saw fruit. Two crimson pomegranates framed by hissing serpents, which had created a tumult in his life some years back and then had sulkily disappeared leaving a gaping blank in his heart. Atchyutanand Gosain fell silent, and cutting through the files of people on both sides, across the rope restraining them, right up to the girl. Standing next to her he whispered in his lost, silent voice, "Najjo... you're Najjo, na?"

In the clamouring surroundings, a new tumult broke loose. This tumult was neither black nor white. The ensuing din too cannot be properly expressed in words. It was an amalgamation of sorts, indicating the making of something new, yet un-formed, therefore a little fluid. That turmoil did not have the soft patter of water, it had noise. It did not seem to refresh, it threatened to wash away; and perhaps because of all this, the girls became exceptionally fearful. With hysterical impatience they pushed Najjo forward. "Let's just get out of here..." they whispered in some haunted tongue. Tripping, falling, they somehow extricated themselves out from the tent. Atchyutanand remained there, rooted to the spot.

The girls decided amongst themselves that they would bury this incident in their breasts and not breathe a word about it, or they would never be allowed to set a foot out alone ever again. "Don't utter a word, or these brothers..."

"Yes..." Najjo grimly thought of her own brothers and agreed. "They shouldn't get a whiff of this."

Maulvi Usman Ali's sudden appearance at this moment felt like an invasion of djinns to the girls. They were dumbstruck. With great trepidation they managed to blurt out, "Assalaamvalekum...." The Maulvi's intrusion into their secret jaunt seemed like a warning, and they doubled up with apprehension.

The next day, in the house that lay near the vacant plot, Najjo struggled to rid her mind of the phantoms chasing her. But time had taken hold of this undesirable matter and was adamant about punishing her, because girls like her could be redeemed only through retribution. There was a family skirmish in progress on TV and Pappu Bhai had to raise his voice over the din, because Najjo would stubbornly never lower the TV's volume, and Ammi never said a thing to her. "Ammi, Maulvi Usmaan Ali was saying that these girls went to see the Devi yesterday. This is sacrilegious. The very shadow of that idol will pervert them."

Najjo shuddered today, just as she had shuddered another

day long back in her childhood. A sudden encounter with inconvenient truths and their consequences can only be unnerving for a young girl. She waited anxiously to hear her mother's response full of a sinking, shrinking feeling. But for all her avowed abidance of the namaz, her mind revolted at the logic of being perverted by the mere shadow of an idol. "How can inanimate things pervert anyone?" She had said it, and now she sat breathlessly awaiting the verdict. She could hear her heart beat, as if throbbing within the fist of a hide and seek game of her childhood gone awry. She just sat, cocooned in a silence which was deeper within than without, and which seemed familiar even though it had surfaced after a long time.

She could feel the texture of every strand in Ammi's voice: "I'll talk to her. She won't go out on her own again." The silence became an unbaked mud pitcher, which shattered within her. A cricket ball had hit it, and it had all happened so surreptitiously that there was no time to gather up the wreckage. If a sob could help gather any shards, it refused utterance. She brooded over Atchyutanand Gosain – how he had bestowed nothing on her except abject humiliation at every juncture. What was this bond between them? He was so distant from her, and yet seemed intent on destroying her life. Why was he everywhere? He was in the vacant plot, on TV, in the marketplace, in the Nav Durga Samiti tent. Between her and her friends, her and her Ammi, her and her brothers and even between her and Maulvi Usman Ali – an obstacle, paving her path with thorns; creating fissures between her and her loved ones. With clenched fists and shaking frame, she stood up, pulled aside the curtain with maroon flowers at the main door and spat out the knot of misery gathering in her gut with as much venom as she could muster.

Now a new etiquette made a forceful entry into Najjo's inner world. The dreams that were a constant part of her existence were perfumed with music as fragrant as sandal scented incense. She gave words to that melody and her heart proclaimed loudly: "Hatred alias Atchyutanand Gosain." He was her other, the one apart, the one who was discussed in whispers around her. She too knew that all these matters had taken birth in her town with the story of some mosque. They all showed it on TV, how people like Atchyutanand Gosain had demolished a mosque in some town called Ayodhya when she was about two. This town too had felt the tremors of that demolition, as had several others in this country in a kind of chain reaction. This sequence, which had begun when she was two, had continued over the years till date. Meanwhile, she too had been growing all these years. Now she had toughened with this new protocol of hatred because it made her more secure and acceptable amongst her own people. Every year on December sixth, from the time she could read, she had read those inscriptions in saffron on the walls in her town: "Ramlalla, we will build a temple there." This phrase never went out of vogue, but would gleam afresh at this time of the year. In her own house every year preparations would be made in advance for December sixth. The curtains would be tightly drawn. Doors would be locked. Kerosene canisters would be stocked and daggers sharpened. Ammi would be overcome with gloom. She didn't know any Babur. She knew very little about Ayodhya or its boundaries. Sitting in this town, what did she care if the mosque remained or was razed...? But Pappu, Guddu and Raja cared. Maulvi Usman Ali made sure that they did. And in this way the difference between them and us would be infused in the air like an essential sentiment in an extremely inflammatory but clandestine manner.

Atchyutanand Gosain lay dozing, sprawled on the wooden couch in Sri Ram Mohan's house. The cards, balloons and dolls strung up in the Archie's showroom in town flashed in his eyes. Heart shaped balloons in red, white and pink. Real hearts capable of bursting with pain! Real hearts utterly broken! He had burst them, wrecked them, with his very own hands this year on February 14, when something called Valentine's Day was being celebrated as the day of love, the day when love could be demonstrated freely. At Sri Ram Mohan's behest, Atchyutanand along with six of his accomplices had landed at that shop and wrecked havoc. All displays of love got a thorough battering that day. He had throttled everything with his own hands. But today, after almost eight months, he recalled those balloons and dolls clearly. That pillaged shop and those hearts...grabbed and popped...

His friends were not familiar with this despondent aspect of Achchu bhaiyaji, as they fondly called him. They tried to tempt him with bottles of chilled beer, but he wouldn't deign to look at them. When Sri Ram Mohan was told about bhaiyaji's plight, he smirked and winked mischievously. Not only was he well aware of the needs of his young aides, he also had adequate provision to fulfil them. "Go take him out for a picture-victure, get him some good booze and make some arrangement." The arrangement could be named Reena, Saira or Meena, and it would be available at the other end of town in some neighbourhood by the railway station. The disciples hoisted bhaiyaji on their shoulders, just as they would during any celebration, and bhaiyaji would twist and turn his neck like a swan and accept all the accolades. But today he just let his body fall limply into the jeep while his friends drove him away in the quest for some pleasurable arrangement.

The Reena, Saira, Meena list was pretty extensive. The arrangements had many valuable assets, and all were served up in gleaming gilded platters to suit bhaiyaji's tastes. But bhaiyaji's body seemed to burn as if he were suffering from sunstroke, and his heart was like a tired sun moving westward, eager to rest. He didn't even look at the offerings. The disciples were worried now. They couldn't fathom what was wrong with him. They finally took him to his elder brother and bhabhi's house to recuperate.

"What happened to Achchu?" asked his bhabhi, surprised to see him back home after so long, in this state. "He is not too well, bhabhi, some kind of fever. We'll get the doctor to check him out tomorrow."

Bhabhi nursed Achchu as well as she could. She rubbed the soles of his feet and his palms with cool oil, massaged his throbbing head, but to no avail. He lay depressed, totally devoid of energy. His face remained lifeless, pale, and shrivelled. Bhabhi called up his disciples: "Seems like he's shadowed by some evil spirits. Get an ojha. He'll exorcise him. He kept muttering 'naj, naj,' the whole night."

"Oh-h...!" The friends were now able to figure out the connection between the 'naj, naj,' chant, the lacklustre face and Achchu bhaiya's withering vitality. They began to complain.

"Kya bhaiya?" grumbled follower Number One.

"Kya bhai...iya?" repeated Number Two.

"Kya bhaiya? You should've given us a hint!" Number Three displayed his exasperation openly.

"Bhaiya, if that is what you wanted, you just had to ask. It wouldn't be difficult to carry her off. In any case, it's a different high, abducting their women. The rascals keep running off with our girls every now and then." Atchyutanand Gosain's limp body convulsed and his eyes blazed like embers. They were already red with fever, but now they began to burn. The fellow who made the comment lost his nerve, he had merely repeated the rhetoric he had been taught in the course of his training.

The fog in Atchyutanand Gosain's mind was assailed by leaping flames. A variety of images would dissolve in it anyhow. He wanted to separate these images and examine them in their different contexts. He wanted to ask Sri Ram Mohan as to what the connection was between the images in the video recordings and this girl who lived in the house next to the vacant plot. None! But he never could ask, because he could not separate and identify them individually.

The disciples let their thoughts gallop on and the remnants of innocence gleamed in the mirrors of their eyes. "Achchu bhaiya's set his heart on that Miyaien!"

The December sixth celebrations this year would

be extraordinary. That Miyaien and her family and her community would be taught a lesson. The rascals are bent upon plaguing Achchu bhaiya. Their mosque was demolished so that they'd get some sense into their heads, but the rascals just don't seem to understand. Keep creating some disturbance or the other...

Sri Ram Mohan, councillor, organised a meeting of his cadres and issued orders to prepare for December sixth a month in advance.

Ammi's heart turned heavy, it hurt, weighed down by gathering anxiety. The thought of arranging Najjo's marriage burgeoned, gnawing at her. Ammi secretly decided on the dates for the engagement and wedding. There was no dearth of proposals for Najjo. But Ammi had to consider each and everything carefully and then arrive at a decision. Prepare for the wedding at the same time. She felt she wouldn't be able to manage all of it in one go, so she thought that she'd begin with getting clothes stitched little by little. Then, maybe she would get some jewellery made. She'd ask her sons to buy household articles like a mixie and a gas stove whenever they went to Delhi, Mumbai. This way a year would just about suffice for getting everything in order, and they'd be saved the trouble of raising funds all at once. She began to visit Agrawal and Sons on a regular basis.

The programme had been set for the night of December fifth. Sri Ram Mohan had issued secret instructions. Not too many, just around three four households had to be done away with, whose sons spoke of pseudo-secularism from the dais of other parties. The rascals always collected weapons at least a week in advance.

There were no special preparations in Najjo's house this year. Pappu and Guddu Bhai were both on duty, and the day of honour for all its colours seemed a little lacklustre this year. This brought some relief to Ammi's troubled heart and Raja too planned to just sleep through his two days' leave from work.

Ammi made up her mind to go and pay off the debt at Agarwal and Sons. True to habit, Najjo began to pester her to be taken along. The same childish obduracy…Ammi just gave her a silent invitation from the corner of her eye. Najjo, the same Najjo, happily tagged along, inseparable as Ammi's shadow. The shop was quite crowded. Sri Ram Mohan councillor's boys were there, directing him to keep the shop closed the next day and join in the procession. The seth heard them out carefully and nodded his head in affirmation. In the midst of all this, the seth noticed Ammi. After all, their association had spanned several years. With his trader's enthusiasm he declaimed, "Please step aside. Let them come in, let the customers come in."

The boys wore spotless white pyjamas. Some shining brows were adorned with a triangular tripund mark. They looked fresh, newly bathed, glowing with vigour and enthusiasm. Hearing him, for a moment they stood still, then shrank back to free a tiny fraction of space. Ammi squeezed through first and was shoved on to the seat meant for customers, followed by Najjo, who true to her childish habit of not letting go her finger, was jostled onto the seat beside her. A nameless disciple of Achchu bhaiya had pushed her there. He watched her intently, as if to ascertain whether this thing he had thrust forward was a mere thing or something that possessed life. His heart jumped into his throat when he realized that this thing was quite alive, a tender being, and it was the very same tender being because of whom poor Achchu bhaiya was burning with fever.

Meanwhile, a rage began to simmer within Najjo. Her dupatta had slipped from her head and now lay on her shoulders. Each face present there seemed to somehow look like the absent Atchyutanand Gosain's face to her. She felt like spewing her pent up rage on that diminutive odious kurta pyjama clad creature who had pushed her. Atchyutanand was there somewhere in him all right. Atchyutanand had so many heads!

However, when the seth had collected his money and was displaying glimmering suit lengths, Najjo's loathing shrank and hid itself. She was charmed by the colours and designs. The shades and textures glowed in her face so that for once even the seth was touched with a feeling like maternal concern. But he checked himself immediately, reverted to his business, and resolved to treat the duo just as customers. He proceeded to scribble a balance of Rs. 2500 in Ammi's account.

By the time Ammi and Najjo stepped out of Agarwal and Sons, the evening shadows had already begun to descend. The market seemed to be in a hurry to close down and head home. Ram Ratan Bartanwala was hurriedly gathering up the glasses, serving bowls and jugs spread outside. Gudiya Bangle Store was readying to shut down. There was a considerable crowd outside O. K. Daily Needs and Jain Bookstore though. There was a smaller crowd outside Alpana Cinema Hall, as there was still some time to go before the nine o'clock show. The chaat-papdi hawkers outside the complex, however, were already leaving. Fewer people went to watch the nine o'clock show. The dewy hint of winter rain rendered the cold breeze even colder. A hazy wintry silence was spreading over the town roads. Ammi's steps were turning brisk and Najjo slowly trailed behind her. Memories of childhood crowded around her. She remembered how she'd walk with Ammi and pester her to tell her stories on the way. She wanted to leap back into the past with Ammi.

"Ammi, this is where the rider used to come, no?"

Ammi did not like her mentioning this. Slowing down she accosted Najjo, "Why are you talking of such things now? Are you out of your mind or what?" Najjo found Ammi's manner strange. Was she so grown-up that she couldn't even talk about her childhood? Najjo remembered how Ammi would narrate stories of this peer who would set out as a rider on such desolate roads on wintry nights. "May Allah have mercy on us! Many people actually saw him face to face. This legend is centuries old and even today travellers have claimed that a lone rider waylaid them with, 'Who? Who are you? Go, go carefully.'"

"Who? Who are you?" a stunted, spotless white kurta pyjama clad figure accosted her. Najjo's mind somersaulted. She wondered how the ghost rider from her childhood tales could have appeared in person. How did the story come alive? Her befuddled eyes tried to make sure, the rider hadn't come on a horse, but in a closed jeep, and he didn't resemble any peer, but the unclean face she'd seen a while ago, in the crowd at Agarwal and Sons. A shudder passed through her entire being, she was too stricken to even cry out. She felt dizzy and fearful of what she saw before her, closed her eyes as if to escape it.

Ammi turned. Had someone called out to her? But when she looked, she found no one calling, nothing at all. The entire scene had melted into silence. She felt as if her motto of trying to stay safe had resolved to betray her today. What was this? Where had her Najjo gone? This was happening in another world, and she should be in a different one. She felt she ought to die. If only she could die by wishing for it... Ammi thought she had found death and began reciting the kalma... "La Illaha Illillaha..." when a heavy object struck her forehead. But as she fell, she definitely saw them force Najjo into that jeep. And leaving behind a huge cloud of smoke and lamentation...the jeep vanished into the black silence of that damp, chilly wind.

The watchman of Nai Duniya Lodge knew all of Sri Ram Mohan's boys. This lodge was about twenty-five kilometres from town. It was a den for the boys as well as a hideaway for Sri Ram Mohan for encounters of the intimate kind. There were just three or four servants and they were perfectly trained. Their job was to serve the boys as unobtrusively as possible. They pretended not to notice them and stayed out of their way. Opened the rooms. Changed bed sheets, put fresh towels in bathrooms, clean water in jugs and then disappeared into their anonymity till summoned again. The gaps beyond these preliminaries did not require their presence or assistance. It was all predetermined.

Atchyutanand Gosain lay in room no. 1 of Nai Duniya Lodge. Before him was a round table with a floral plastic cover, blossoming with red flowers. A half empty whiskey bottle was placed on it with a half empty glass lying in a slapdash manner beside it. Prone on the bed, Atchyutanand glanced at them again and again, wondering why he didn't like whiskey any more, or why it didn't hit him as it used to with that slow, simmering intoxication. Just then, two of his followers barged into the room, their arms and shoulders supporting a limp, half-falling shape. This shape seemed to resemble that of Najjo's, which occupied his thoughts so. But how? He sat up with a start and saw that this shape had been laid next to him with a pillow under its head. He suddenly experienced an overwhelming high. He glanced down with his inebriated eyes – the pomegranates glowed all right. The shape seemed to be alive, throbbing with life. He wondered how? It was his mind conjuring it all up. Disappointed, he laughed like a crazed man. It was all an illusion, all of it. Seeing Achchu Bhaiya laugh after so many days, the disciples felt heartened and said, overjoyed, "It's a gift for you, Bhaiya. Unwrap it tomorrow. Goodnight!"

Achchu bhaiya thumped the bed with a childlike artlessness and stammered, "Saale…behen… Is this real or is it a dream? Can't seem to figure out anything?"

"Bhaiyaji, it's real, absolutely real, we swear! Go ahead, touch her…" And with this they were out of the room.

After they left, Atchyutanand Gosain re-entered the fog of his mind once again, to make sense of this development. What had these guys done? Had they really? He decided to touch the shape beside him to confirm whether it was real or just a dream… What? First, he tried to assess the heat in those searing pomegranates. His fingers trembled and when he touched them, he singed his hands. He was confused and angry. First of all he had burnt his hands and secondly, the hissing serpents framing the pomegranates were nowhere to be seen. He gathered his fingers together to pinch the shape's arm forcefully and elicited a faint cry. "Ahh…" A voice seemed to come from afar, soft, faint, and stuck to the walls like a spider. Atchyutanand was overjoyed. His dream had a voice. It had traversed a long distance to reach him and had finally become true.

Passers-by on that desolate stretch brought Ammi back to consciousness. She had fallen in the middle of the road, but found herself on the side when she arose. Her helplessness stabbed her painfully. She wanted to cry out loud, "Hai! My Najjo!" but thinking of her daughter's honour, she wept silently. She allowed herself to sink into that abyss within her, which had occupied such a huge space at the time of her husband's demise. The passage of time had slowly filled it up, but today it had brazenly excavated even greater depths. It was tearing at Ammi with the knowledge of its existence, along with her sobs…

"What happened?" "Arre, look what has happened!" "Behenji, what happened? Did the hooligans rob you of anything?" "Yes, yes, yes…No! No!"

A scooterist passing by was stopped and Ammi was transported to Rajiv Nagar. Beside herself, Ammi rushed towards the house in frenzy. Raja was sitting outside with a group of friends. "Najjo!" Ammi cried out, and collapsed. Before the entire incident could be figured out, the boys had armed themselves and were all set to avenge the dishonour.

Maddened, Ammi cried out, "Arre, how will this fighting help me find Najjo? Inform the police first...."

The boys became furious. Anger and humiliation brought tears to Raja's eyes. "Let us wipe them out today. The whole lot of them!" he roared.

Ammi began to lose ground despite the logic of her arguments, and began to plead, "Police, ask for the police's help!" The boys left her, setting off to enlist other youngsters from Rajiv Nagar in their campaign. Necessary preparations for such encounters had in any case been under way. Driven out of her wits, Ammi staggered to the stuffy room at the end of the house. A trunk covered with pink flowers and green leaves still lay there, where long back, little Najjo had been temporarily lost when she tried to climb on top of it.

Ammi began to search for Najjo's footprints in the half darkness.

Atchyutanand couldn't believe his luck. He wanted to scream and call out to Najjo with the full intensity of his passion, "Najjo is that really you, so close to me?" But he couldn't. Suddenly he caught sight of the two black serpents, seeking whom he had lost himself a while ago. They sat with their hoods poised right in front him, ready to strike. Even though he was still riding high on his triumph, he faltered for a moment. He bent to confront the visage of the shape, which had by now emerged from the shadow to turn completely into Najjo's face. When it did that something slimy and repulsive spattered on his face and seemed determined to enter him through his mouth. He began to feel awful. He pulled out a handkerchief from his pocket and wiped Najjo's face and then his own. He heard some fractured words spill out of Najjo's mouth and tried to focus his mind and ears on them. When he joined those scattered words together, the hate-filled emotion suffusing them became apparent. The poisonous barbs, too, were obvious. He was surprised – how could such a lovely, delicate girl harbour such venom? His mind exhausted itself trying to figure out all these new developments. To find some relief, he changed his position. He plonked himself in the chair beside the bed in an attempt to gauge Najjo's sentiments. Suddenly he heard the clock ticking. The sound brought back memories of all the video films he had seen at Sri Ram Mohan's house. That vandalized mosque, and the thousands of kar sevaks milling around, people atop the mosque and the cries, "Give it one more push!" His whole being was aroused, and he rose to meet the challenge. Voices clamoured and jumbled up in his mind yet again. The ticking of the clock, the changing times, the commencement of a new day, the creation of a new world...the whole earth shook with the sound of those words and out came the sun, flaunting itself, as it saluted the anniversary of the victorious dawn.

*Translated* by *Anu Jaidev*

# The Hunt

*Pratyaksha*

Her body reeked of the odour of yeasty dough, warm, moist, slightly sour. Especially the portion of her stomach that was visible between her blouse and her sari. Like a well kneaded mound of fine dough.

The tablecloth was spread in front of me. Bakarkhani roti with mutton curry. Bowls spilling over with sweet rice and pudding. I was breaking off pieces of bread and dipping it in the curry and as I ate, I stole furtive looks at her. She watched me eat, silently. Unknowingly, helplessly, my eyes slipped from her face to her uncovered stomach. The corner of her lace bordered sari had slipped away revealing the white mound of her soft navel. I had learnt that women of her age, no longer in the first flush of youth, women in their thirties, become a little careless, a little less conscious of their bodies. Younger, unmarried girls, are extremely aware of their bodies. Even if they wish to reveal themselves, they do it with an air of alert consciousness that emanates like a scent from each and every pore of their fresh skins. The mindful aroma of the come hither look. If they wish to conceal, it is as if yards of cloth hide them like a mysterious shroud and at the same time open up the sensuous revelation like a slow, deep sigh. But women in their thirties, their saris slipping away from the generous swell of their rounded bosoms, the delicate killing curve of a filled-out back, the ample eroticism of the flesh between the stomach and the waist, the swelling fertile roundness bearing evidence of their having borne a child, scorch like a searing flame. Oh boy, these ripe, in-their-thirties women.

I watched her as I ate. Her eyes were shadowed with the black magic of the previous night. It did not look as if she had freshened her eyes with kohl in the morning. It was as if they revealed the night's sorcery and the morning bore witness to its dark spells. Her eyes were not really beautiful. But I found them so. They were small, slanting, shiny, black, luminescent eyes, shaded with dark, dense lashes. As if hiding a deep mystery, holding it within, like the restless surface of the water, just a moment before the ripples die down, like a still frozen pond amidst the dense jungle, reflecting the dark green outlines of the trees around.

I continued to watch her. The diamond nose pin flashed its fire. It shouldn't have, because she sat still. But I fidgeted. My eyes were filled with the leaping flames of the diamond's fire. Her hands nestled in her lap, quiet, still. Pink cuddly palms. Lotus flower palms. She would have cooked the mutton with these hands. I was full now, satiated. She pushed the bowl of kheer towards me silently. Then she wrapped her pallu around her shoulders with utmost care, tucking it securely at her waist. Had she become aware of my wandering, yearning glances? I sat up, alert and conscious.

The other day when I dropped in, I found a flurry of activity. I sat in the back room with Rafiq. Abbu's accounts had to be checked. The adjacent veranda bustled with festivity. Something was cooking in a large pot. Clouds of steam rose from it. The fragrance of food, the aroma of spices being sautéed. The clatter of plates and utensils. The music of the ladle scraping the sides of the pan. The small pile of thinly sliced onions. Rafiya, moving busily, touching this and picking up that. Khadima, with her dupatta around her head, pulverizing fresh spices on the grinding stone, muttering with annoyance under her breath all the while. And amidst all this, she sat in the centre, calm, on a low stool. She had wrapped her dupatta around her head. Not a single strand of hair was visible. Her face was pink, flushed from the heat of the stove.

- Come, let's sit in the sun. Rafiq picked up the bundle of papers.

The chairs were pulled out. A round table was set in the middle. It was covered with a white lace tablecloth. Then tea was served in tall glasses. Spiced, milky, well-brewed tea. It was time for the zohar namaz. You could hear the call of the muezzin. Rafiq's abbu got up, pulled out the janamaz, the prayer mat, knelt on his knees and began the prayers. I tilted my chair towards the veranda. Red chillies were being sautéed in the oil. They would be ground to a fine paste later. In a separate pan, thin slivers of onion were being fried for the biryani.

- Rafiya, move your hands faster

- Khadima bring a plate, a spoon too

Her voice had a balanced stillness. Khadima, muttering with annoyance, moved away from the grinder, hitched her salwar further up her calf and entered the kitchen.

- Would you like to taste the bageri? It is almost cooked.

When I was a child the bageriwala often used to come to our house. The flat round woven baskets filled up with chattering birds, bageri or yellowhammers, snipes, partridges, quail. They would be bought by the dozen. The piteous chirping of the birds filtered through the slits in the basket.

- Hey kid, why don't you move to the other side?

The bageriwala would admonish me while he put his hand through the narrow slit in the wicker flap and pulled out the hapless birds one by one, wringing their necks in one swift stroke and piling them up in a heap. Then he would call for a bucket of water and the dead birds would be dunked in it, their feathers pulled out. I would run away then, nauseated at the sight, vowing to myself, that I'd never touch a morsel of bageri, ever. Then the bageri would be cooked, with the oil separating from the spices in a thin circle, a delicate flavoured pattern at the edge of the white bone china platter and I would end up eating four rotis instead of my normal daily quota of two. Then, the bageriwala stopped coming and I was freed from the intense moral dilemma of eating a bageri.

And today, after such a long time? The aroma of cinnamon and cloves and cardamom rose in the air with a sharp insistence. Bay leaves, sticks of cardamom and pieces of cloves were being tied up in a piece of muslin and placed in the pot of rice. The spiky fumes rising from the frying red chillies singed my eyes and seared my throat, making me cough. The cooked bageri was placed before me. Wrapped in spices, the oil seeping away from it. Brazenly looking deep into her eyes, I swallowed the portion in one go. The sting of the spices brought tears into my eyes, but I continued to gaze at her. Her face reddened. There was embarrassment, a hint of shame, and some hauteur. All flashed on her face, a strange amalgam of emotions. She stood still for a while as if confused, then turned, disappearing into the kitchen.

I was becoming more impudent as the days went by. More audacious. A compulsive brashness impelled me. She had begun to hesitate to appear before me. But by this time I had become a part of the household. I had access now to the women's inner courtyard. Ammi, meaning the Badi Begum would ask me to come inside and sit with them. She would slice thin slivers of betel nut with her nutcracker, the paandaan would be laid open. Her hair was coloured with henna to a brownish red and age was weaving a spider's web on her dazzlingly fair face.

- Mahrukh beta, why don't you offer him the sevaiyan you made yesterday?

I would eat, my eyes fixed on hers. She was like a trapped bird gazing at me hypnotized. She would open her mouth as if about to refuse Ammi's request. Then she would purse her lips. I had become extremely cunning in this matter. My face would reflect innocence, carelessness. Only my eyes would convey their message. My restless eyes that roamed over her lips, her breasts, her palms nestling quietly in her lap. A searing flame rose within me, slowly heightening my fever. She had become very aware of me, quite vigilant. She would keep herself properly wrapped up. In front of me, she would constantly be fidgeting with her dupatta, her fingers would move from her hair to her face in short, sharp, restless movements. She would sweep strands of invisible hair back from her face, wipe a face already clean. Now she was awkward and unsure in my presence. Her anger was replaced by restless bashfulness. I had chosen my prey with care. Her husband, Ashraf, was away and came home maybe once a year. But in all justice it had to be said that I was the hunted, the original victim. It was later that I turned hunter. It was a pre-planned conspiracy. A complete conspiracy. Now I was on the look-out for an opportunity.

It had all begun like this – I had merely looked at her. But, when our eyes met, I flushed and turn away. Her face flashed a small knowing smile. She turned aside hiding her laughter. Then, as the game progressed, my gaze turned brazen. I would look her straight in the eye. Now *she* had become jittery. The more panicky she became, the more unabashed did I get. It was all a game for me, a mere game – to see her reduced to such a state, to rob her of her disdain, her haughtiness. A fermenting yearning attraction, but still, merely a game.

A throbbing desire to drown in this fragrant swamp would flare up. My restless energy was beginning to reach out to her. In my presence she was like a frightened, trapped animal, impatient, unsure. Her fingers trembled as they moved over her face, hair, clothes, sweeping, smoothing, scattering, restless, awkward, trembling fingers. In spite of the cold, a sheen of sweat filmed her face. On mine spread the smug anticipation of trapping my prey.

And finally, my time came. That day I was in Rafiq's room. She had entered with a bundle of clothes in her arms. The room was dark. The electricity had just gone and Rafiq had gone to arrange for some light. I could sense her shadow in the dark. Then, a sweet cinnamon-like scent. I crept up on that fragrance from behind, clasped it. I gathered up the velvet darkness, held it to my heart, filled my eyes with it, touched my lips to it. A smoke rose, solid, yet flowing, a wild creeper, a jasmine flower. O my love! A groan slipped out and then something unexpected happened. A tight, sharp slap turned my face awry.

How could I have been so wrong? How could the prey turn into the hunter even as it was dying? Defiance? I ran from the house like a thief. Then vanished from the scene for several days. A couple of times when I happened to come across Rafiq, I made some excuse.

Sitting in the train I kept thinking of all this. From the barred windows I could see villages rushing along, fields lush and green, half-naked urchins running along the track with the train till the speed left them behind panting, hens with their chicks in front of small huts, cackling with sudden alarm at the sound of the train, buffaloes lying languid in ponds, a long line of quacking ducks, rows and rows of palm trees, villagers watering fields with Persian wheels. All these flashed before my eyes. I craned my neck, resting my forehead against the iron bars, trying to hold on to the images till the last minute possible. One village would appear, get left behind, then another, then another. Field after field, meadows after meadow, small hamlets, one or two cyclists, a family sitting in a tractor trailer at the railway crossing, waiting patiently for the train to pass by. I sat numb, sipping intermittently at tea in earthen cups. Nibbling sweets, peanuts roasted in hot sand, spicy gram. Passengers kept buying and munching. The floor of the compartment was littered with peanut shells and empty paper packets.

The shoe polish boy kept shining shoes. The blind beggar drummed on his aluminium plate as he sang bhajans. And, amidst all this hullabaloo, I sat unmoved and numb. Swaying with the rhythm of the train, dozing. My head kept banging against the bars in the window. When I woke up the bump that had swelled as a result brought a throbbing pain above my ear. I jerked the thoughts away. The thoughts of anger, embarrassment, shame and defeat, above all else, defeat.

The gauna would take place this time – the bride was to be brought home. At home – piles of yellow dhotis, the courtyard filled with papads, badis drying and pickle maturing in the sun. Hordes of relatives. The front yard canopied for guests to sit. Cooks on the terrace. Puris puffing in boiling oil, crisp imartis, fried parwals, boiled potato and pea curry, boondis in curd. The sacred fire, rituals, chanting of mantras. Hustle and bustle, to-ing and fro-ing. Playing children, women decking up. Feet decorated with aalta, toe-rings and nose-rings. Winnowing baskets filled with rice, coconut and turmeric. Pandits, the barber and the go-between. I forgot everything. Everything.

I could recall only her coy presence. Her gold-edged red shawl tied to my turmeric yellow wrapper. Like a shy bundle, she entering the house for the first time, behind me, placing her feet one after the other in the winnowing basket, following the age old ritual of a bride entering her husband's house for the first time. The welcome with the betel leaf. The auspicious rice, the vermilion powder, turmeric and curd.

Then we were alone, just the two of us.

I bolted the door. The yellow bundle was on the bed. The room was heavy with the fragrance of turmeric and sandal. My palms were damp. I put a thumb beneath her chin and lifted her face. Thick, shiny eyebrows and beneath them, closed eyes shadowed with thick lashes. Beneath the trembling nose ring, her full lips. Aah!

The dozens of green and yellow bangles had slipped to her elbows from her delicate slender wrists, as if she had put on some one else's. What size bangles did she wear? I clasped her wrists to assess their thickness but she shrank back shyly. A pulse trembled at her collar bones for a moment. The delicate tiny hollow between them shivered, sobbed, then beat a nervous tattoo. I gathered the bundle in my arms. She trembled with an unknown emotion. I was afraid that if I held her too tight, my patience would shatter into a thousand pieces. The sweet smell of fresh milk, the first rain drops on fresh earth. The drip-drip patter of water in small puddles then the heavy downpour. The raw green freshness of tender grass, raw then green, then sweet, oh, so sweet.

Something grazed my palms. I saw that it was the khoincha, the customary rice and turmeric root tied in the corner of her sari to bring auspicious blessings. It was waiting for some naughty sister-in-law to open the knot and take out the rice. But who was there at my house? No sister-in-law, no sister, no brother's wife. My elder brother had remained single. Never married. Why, no one knows. But so tall and well-built... And then the whispers – the murmurs of impotency. But whatever it was, apart from Amma there was really no one else in the house who could open the khoincha.

Then I had to take on the role. My fingers suddenly became clumsy. I fumbled with the first knot. Then once the first knot loosened everything fell open. The rice, the turmeric root, the sprig of grass, the crumpled fifty-rupee note and the one-rupee coin. Everything scattered in a heap.

In the morning, while bathing at the tube well, the sweet heavy smell of mahua filled my pores. Dark viscous honey dripped in my veins. This time, when I went back, it was in an altogether different mind frame.

But I continued to visit their place. The second beginning also happened in a strange fashion. Rafiq almost dragged me home this time. My friendship with Rafiq dated back many years. It was the kind of friendship punctuated with minor squabbles followed with reconciliation. Sometimes he would ask for a loan with such a righteous authority that I had to borrow the money from elsewhere for him. If ever I refused him he would say, will you give it or not? If he needed it, who else would he turn to except me? At times the moment I spoke there would be arguments. He would go off in a huff. Then return and ask to be appeased.

Sometimes he would invite me for breakfast and fob me off with plain bread and omelette, saying with innocent charm that he would offer biryani and kebab some other time.

It was not that we were young kids anymore but our bickering was like that. Ammi, Ashraf bhai, everyone in the household, even Khadima, Rafiya and the children would laugh affectionately at us, indulge us. Such friendship, such guileless friendship. On the night of 31st December we sat drinking, languid and intoxicated, reminiscing about long forgotten things, steeped in a tipsy feeling of brotherhood. We repeated over and over – you are my chum, you are my bro, in the way drunk people always do, treading the same old path, faithfully meticulous. Later on, when we sobered down, the others teased us. We smiled sheepishly at our ridiculously emotional behaviour.

We often had heated arguments on each and every issue. There was no difference. We were like two people lost in their own world, totally unaware of their surroundings. Over countless cups of tea and pakoras we would argue till the night fell, not caring which side the other took. We were in opposition, of course, but enchanted by the power of our own logic, our words would burn with passion. At such times we would slip from one side to the other with ease, riding over words, emotions, logic and in the end, dead tired, we would trudge back home.

Then why, inexplicably setting aside this precious friendship, jeopardizing it in fact, why did I turn towards her? Just like a snake hypnotizes, her small, slanting shiny eyes had mesmerized me. But what happened, happened for the best. It was truly for the best. The only problem was that I became uncomfortable in her presence. I would try to avoid meeting her by confining myself to the front portion of the house. If she ever came there, I would immediately leave. That tingling slap would flash before me. My palms would automatically rise to stroke my cheek. So it was good that nothing happened that day. I was saved from drowning in a swamp that day. Saved to keep on meeting Rafiq. Saved for the sweet, pure untouched smell of turmeric and the heavy fragrance of mahua.

But, then, I began to notice that her eyes were on me all the time. What was she waiting for – an apology? A kind of expectation actually seemed to spread over her face. Her eyes would open just a little wider as if goading me to say something, anything. But what could I say? A feeling of shame drowned me. All I could think of was a yellow bundle and the sweet, raw green smell of grass.

All the time, something throbbed like a beating heart, waiting to happen. Waited in the zarda and keema, in the shammi and reshami kebab, in the fragrant spicy betel nut, in the attar and perfume, in the open courtyard, in the veranda, in the clothes left to dry on thin wire hangers, in the enormous legs of the salwars, in the lace-edged dupattas, in the narrow legs of the churidaar pyjamas, in bangles and birds, in the doves and the canaries. And one day that waiting placed its lips on my neck below my ears, hot and searing. A wound, burning like a flashing fire. As if the hawk had dived sharply on its prey. I was caught. My breath went berserk, my arms and legs floundered. I was truly trapped. The hunter was caught in his own snare.

The thick dense honey began to flow in my veins. Sweet,

heavy and sticky, and I went down under. It was an eddy, a maelstrom and I was sucked in like a hapless twig. A heavy blanket of fragrance was spread over me and my breath came in short, gasping pants. My legs buckled under the onslaught of passion. I forgot everything, everything.

So many years have passed now. So many long years. Everything was left behind. The town, all my friends. My body has lost all its music, all rhythm. My heart has become dry and dull. Nothing stirs it now. There is no colour left in my life. My mind does not go crazy any more, not after any damn thing. The dull routine of running the house, the monotony of chores and the routine of bringing up children. There is no joy anymore, anywhere – a dull oppressiveness in the business of living and it has sapped me, wrung me dry.

That day though, I saw a strange thing in my neighbourhood. This bumpkin – God knows from which corner of some far-flung village – he had a basket hung from a stick across his shoulders. His clothes were dusty, his shoes dry and misshapen and his face was an advertisement for dust-stained sweatiness. God knows what was inside the wicker basket. Some tawdry goods or knick-knacks or who knows some magical Pandora's box. He walked along, gazing with wide, astonished eyes at his surroundings. I stopped short in my tracks. There must have been a flicker of a smile on my face definitely because when my eyes met his there was the slow beginning of a response, a little abashed, like the parody of a smile flashing briefly. Then, in a fraction of a second, the man disappeared from view, was lost in the milling crowd. One breath ago he was within the range of my sight and by the time I drew the next, he had vanished completely. I took a deep breath and believe me, I didn't just breathe in plain air but a strong whiff of cooked bageri, fragrant with cardamoms, cinnamon and cloves – a delicious morsel of bageri. Who would believe it – but the taste actually spread from the tip of my tongue and filled my mouth. And with it flashed a tender hot scar of waiting, on my neck below my ears – a tiny tongue of flame.

Till now I'm not sure who had hunted whom.

*Translated by Pratyaksha*

# *Transformation*

*Kavita*

I have left Ma in her new world and I am on my way back.

Life sometimes brings us to a point where our roles are transformed. I was at such a point in my life today.

In every journey, there are other parallel journeys. I'm returning after leaving Ma in her new world, then why is Ma travelling with me? Why has the journey of my going to her become a part of this return? We are both on our own journeys; Ma is going back and I forward. What is wrong? Don't the earth and the sky and planets revolve on their own axes? Rivers also change course, then why expect Ma to be the epitome of boundless patience? Why must she remain unmoving at this turning point all her life when she did not ask for it? All of us have taken steps forward on our journeys, but Ma must remain in stillness, fixed as she waits for us. Ma was not a mountain and mountains too erode with time. All too human, she felt happy and sad, felt fear and pain, disgust and anger, even as we forgot something that was so self-evident. Even then, all of us wished that Ma should remain unmoving, still as the mountain.

In my childhood, it was she who would narrate this story of the early days of creation. Bacteria, worms and insects, water and land, mud and sky and plants – God must have created humans after that. They all had their own momentum and their own courses. At that time, the sun and the moon decided to exchange their jobs and their character. The moon would be free of its cool temperament and the sun would no longer have to bear the terrible heat everyday. The next day would surely be miraculous for them as they would have moved far from the humdrum dailiness of their lives. In a new life... there was only pleasure ahead.

But this little exchange was disastrous for all creation. People suffered from the unbearable heat every night, unable to sleep. Instead, the day brought sleep so that all work came to a standstill. A day passed...then another...this change seemed permanent. This little exchange brought a hurricane, an earthquake in the realm of creation. All such notions as day-night, hunger-thirst, life-death began to lose their meaning. It was as if God had cursed them...

How could you forget this story? You would recite Kabir's inversions and their meaning would find expression in your life and now you go and invert everything? Such crashing waves in the ocean of your life? Ma, why were you like the ocean...you knew these breakers would not just dash against you, they would set up a tsunami in all our lives. And it was like that in our family. You shrugged and our world was rocked to the core.

I really missed you Ma, missed you so terribly. Anuj sensed this and would say, "Call Ma. Find out how she is doing." How could I diminish his generosity by telling him that if I called, it would only bring my helplessness home to me? My bounds and incapacities would emerge, with their mouths wide open ready to devour me. What if I found that Ma was ill…where would I be then?

That night the phone rang insistently. My fear held my palms captive. Who could it be at this hour? Anuj woke up. "Pick up the phone, Appu." Now that he was by my side, I steeled myself for any eventuality…

"Hello…"

"Is that Appu?"

"Yes, this is Appu. Bhabhi, so late at night, what is the matter…?"

The trembling inside showed up in my body and in my voice. Anuj sat up.

"What is it?"

"Nothing much but you must take the first train tomorrow and come here."

The first train…I felt tears in my throat. "Bhabhi, I hope Ma is well. When did you get there?"

"Ma is all right. The entire family is here. You must come tomorrow."

No further inquiries were possible as the phone was disconnected. I fell on the bed as Anuj put his arms around me to support me. "What happened, Appu?"

"I don't know. She says that Ma is fine but I must come tomorrow. Is that possible, Anuj?"

"Oh, they hadn't visited home for so long, they must all have planned this trip together. So they asked you to come too. Why worry so much?"

In the morning, Anuj somehow packed for me and as he put me on the train, he said, "Come back soon Appu. You know how difficult it is for me to stay without you even for a day." The train moved and Anuj's hands, holding on to mine through the window, pulled away first and then slowly his image receded. As soon as he vanished from sight, the image of Ma appeared – what could have happened to her that everybody had gathered there and I wasn't informed? I scolded myself fiercely for the tears dimming my eyes. It is inauspicious to cry like this. Nothing has happened to Ma, or else Bhabhi would have told me…?

Bhabhi! Even though she's in the same city, she has been living in her mother's rabbit warren of a house for a year and not with Ma. And my brother doesn't say a word, Ma's favourite younger son. There had been no place for her in the households of her older sons in any case. The sons felt that it was better this way…but this did not mean that they did not love Ma. Whenever they came, they would employ new servants for her comfort. They would give her lots of money and buy all kinds of things for the house. All for her and for her well-being, isn't it? But did that take care of the loneliness…?

I had called once and the phone rang for a long time. Why wasn't anybody picking it up…one…two…four rings…I was just about to disconnect when I heard a faint voice at the other end… "Hello…who is it?"

"It's Appu. Why is your voice sounding so weak? Why weren't you picking up the phone? What happened?"

"I fell down in the courtyard this morning."

"You fell? Why didn't you call me? Are you all right? Any bones broken…?"

"No, just a slight sprain… I couldn't get up from bed. That is why I took so long to get to the phone."

"Have you been to a doctor?"

"Who is there to take me? I paid the neighbour's sweeper to apply turmeric and lime. It'll get better by and by…"

"The neighbour's sweeper, but where is Debu, your servant?"

"Oh, he ran away a long time ago. He even stole that watch of your father's, the one kept near his photograph, and some money…"

"Did you file a complaint?" I checked myself. Who would have filed a complaint? "And your part-time maid?"

"She left two months ago saying her granddaughter was getting married and she may not return as her daughter will be all alone after the marriage."

Mothers care so deeply for their daughters, I thought to myself, and daughters…? Ma was still speaking.

"Ma, what did you eat?"

"The neighbour brought some khichdi. Half of it is left over. I'll eat it if I feel like it."

Would Anuj let me go? But why ask? Ma doesn't like me to leave Anuj behind and stay with her. Never has he said, "Let us bring Ma here. She can stay with us for a few days."

Not once. If Anuj loves her so much then why doesn't he understand? Doesn't he remember that my brothers had opposed our marriage and if we did get married it was only because of Ma's staunch support. Anuj's middling job, his ordinary looks were all bones of contention for my brothers. And the biggest stumbling block was that he was Apoorva's own choice. What will people say, 'Just because she didn't have a father, three brothers couldn't find a suitable match for their only sister.'

Ma was the one who stood firm. Anyone who wants to come can come – else let them stay away. Everyone is free to think whatever he or she likes. I have respected the dreams and desires of all my children. Just like my sons, Apoorva has the right to her own choices in life and I will stand by her.

How would she have swallowed that stale khichdi, Ma who always disliked tasteless food? Laughter, colour and taste were all things that were an intrinsic part of her life but they have all vanished now. Ma disliked saris in pale colours but since father died, she'd had to wear only white saris. Fish was her favourite food but now there was only vegetarian fare. Even in her daughter-in-law's bland offerings she'd manage to infuse taste with a little curd here, a dash of pickle or chutney.

Tears welled up and I furtively wiped my eyes. If any of the passengers saw me crying, what would they think? I just wanted Ma to be fine. I would bring back all her lost pleasures, her forgotten delights and all the promises I'd made to her.

I am flooded with past memories. After my wedding,

when I went to meet her for the first time, I had many albums of honeymoon photographs. She said to me before sundown, "Let me see them first. All the others can see them later but I won't be able to see much without sunlight." Ma had had cataract for years. But nobody thought of an operation. She still keeps stitching and embroidering little things. Even if she gets a bad headache later. In spite of a bad case of gout, she still does the housework and walks without any support. "Why don't you just sit down quietly? Let the others know that you are suffering. If you just keep on bearing the pain and not tell anybody, how will they find out? Just stop doing all the work and then see if anybody else takes over." I'd complain.

Ma would reply calmly, "I am getting on, there are bound to be aches and pains. If I just sit around and do nothing, my body will rust and then I'll be dependent even for a glass of water. All these afflictions are meant tell you that old age is about to come swooping down soon."

Perhaps such arguments led to a situation where Ma began to limp and years went by and she continued to limp. Her eyes were getting worse too, but we brothers and sisters had stopped taking notice. We had begun to see these changes as a part of her personality.

So we were talking about my pictures... Ma spread out a durrie in the courtyard and laid the pictures around her. She looked at each one with great attention, taking note of everything. Her interest was childlike, "People must be getting wet when the waves come...I wonder how it feels...?"

It was as if she was talking to herself and I did not hear

her remarks as a query. Even as they echoed in my mind, "These mountains look small in these photographs. How do they look when you are closer to them? You must get dwarfed by them…?" Ma continued her soliloquy.

I slid back into the voices of my childhood and spoke, "I'll take you there, Ma. This time you must come with me and…" The yawning distance between what I wanted and what I could do was all too real. My joy and my precious memories weighed me down with shame. Ma had never been to big cities, never seen big rivers, never watched breakers in an ocean, never touched a mountain and now…I felt sad and helpless. Why can't I fulfil my childhood promise, "When I grow up, I'll fly a big, big plane and take you everywhere?"

My wings were newly sprouted then and I slipped in and out of the dreams of my future home with Anuj. Where was there time to study so that I could keep my promise to Ma? This happens when you are in love. Old promises fade way in the face of new ones.

If I confided in Anuj in a moment of sadness, all that he would say is, "What sort of brothers do you have…they all have such fine jobs, they should take Ma on a trip. She is getting old now, so if nothing else, at least they could take her on a pilgrimage…" As if the responsibility of Ma's happiness was only to be borne by her sons.

Why was I thinking about Ma these past few days? I understood the reason only after I got to her. Ma had stirred in her sleep and the sheet had slipped off her face and the bed. Her face looked like that of an innocent dreaming baby. After Papa's death, when had her face looked so calm? I switched off the light.

I got off silently at the platform. I took a rickshaw. Even though I had come here after a long time, why did it feel as if we were all here and always had been? Everything was so familiar, nothing seemed to have changed. It felt the same way with Ma. As if we had always been with her.

I tightened my fists over the worms of anxiety, refusing to acknowledge them. The neighbourhood appeared quiet and so did our house. I alighted from the rickshaw quietly. No, if there was bad news, the house could not be so quiet. No crowd of people, no movement, no voices. But the silence was also disquieting. There were so many people in the house, children too, and still not a sound…I opened the gate. Bade Bhaiya comes to the door, "Come Apoorva. Hope your journey was comfortable. We've all been waiting for you."

I take note of how much Bade Bhaiya looks like my father. Greying at the temples, a certain heaviness in his frame, the same eyes. Even his voice sounds the same. He never used to look like my father, this change has come suddenly…

Ma was not to be seen in the sitting room. I bent down uneasily to pay my respects to all the elders. "Bhabhi, Ma?" Ma must be in the kitchen. A wave of relief…but then an odd feeling…I had arrived and no sign of Ma to hug me joyfully. This was a first. "I'll go and meet Ma…give me two minutes," I said as I made my way to the kitchen.

Bhaiya's grim face and deep voice arrested my feet. "Apoorva, you can meet Ma and talk to her. That is why we called you here. But not so fast. Listen to what we have to say."

"Tell me." I did try and keep sarcasm out of my voice. I dive into myself and think that Ma must be ill and these people must want to take her with them and Ma's bitter memories must not let her agree. They must want me to persuade Ma. They all think that Ma listens to me...but what will I say to her and how?

"Appu, are you listening? I was saying that Ma wants to get married." He emphasized 'married'. That emphasis hit me like a hammer on my head. Something clanged in my brain. I was wrenched out my reverie.

"What?"

"Yes, Ma is going to get married...and I...I mean all of us don't see why she needs to do this? Let her spend her last years in peace and comfort. In a few years, she'll be marrying off her grandchildren."

"Ma's gone senile," murmured Chhoti Bhabhi, "all of you live elsewhere so you won't be affected. We live in the same town. We'll lose face completely."

I was in shock as I listened. "Whose marriage?" I asked to confirm.

"Her marriage, who else? She is sure to listen to you. You must talk her out of this. If she feels lonely here, our wives will take turns to stay with her for four months each. Or else, if she is willing to stay with us by turn, that is even better."

I thought that Ma had initiated a new game to get her children back into her life so that the silence in her life would be filled with the sounds of domesticity again. Why shouldn't I join her game quietly, "So your wives will stay here, but what about the children?"

"Well, they can't be expected to give up their schooling. And there are no really good schools here. But we'll surely bring them over in the holidays."

"Will you be able to look after the children without the Bhabhis for four months?

"Yes, and what choice do we have? At least we'll be able to save our honour. If Ma gets married at this age, we'll be left with no face to show."

"If Ma is getting married now, it is because she is lonely, not because she can't win over her body's needs, Bhaiya. Then why worry about having no face to show? Whatever dreams we had, Ma fulfilled them. She stood by each of us in all our decisions and today when she's all alone and has never complained about it...she has expressed one desire and this is all we can say in response? How many years does she have left? Ten, may be fifteen. If she lives out these years happily and we too don't have to worry about her well-being because she is alone...there can be no harm in that?"

"At an age when people go on pilgrimages or turn to religion, for a woman with grandchildren to marry...I've never heard of something so bizarre. Pitaji's soul must be hurting to see this..."

"I don't know if there is a soul or not, if there is, then it must have hurt equally to see the children she doted upon, turn away from her. You can't live your life only with memories. Perhaps Pitaji's soul will be at peace to see that Ma is well...that there is somebody with her to share her joy and sorrow." I stopped, amazed to feel the angry heat on my face.

I confront my elder brothers in this fashion. Bhabhi has quietly left...perhaps I should not have spoken with such bitterness. I notice that the pain on my middle brother's face has lessened though he still looks disturbed. There is a tinge of uncertainty when he speaks as if he were considering my words.

"If Pitaji were here, we would have celebrated their golden wedding anniversary shortly. If we had celebrated it according to custom, it would have been like a marriage with all the ceremonies. We would not have resented that... After completing all her duties, Ma has only asked for some years for herself. That too of her own life."

My younger brother seemed to be arguing with himself. I was glad that my voice had had an effect on one of them at least. When we were younger, he'd always listen to me and our views were often similar. The two of us were the more emotional and sensitive ones. That is why we did not go as far as the two older brothers. But his wife gave him less respect because he didn't think only of himself. When the two older ones were aiming high elsewhere, he stayed on to support and look after Ma while he studied. She would be amused and irritated with him by turns. According to Bhabhi, he was a fool and she was suffering the consequences.

"If for a moment, we imagine that it was Pitaji instead of Ma, we might have been willing to consider the idea...but Ma...never. But who is he? What does he do...where did she meet him? Will someone tell me?"

"The question is not who he is and what he is like. The question is that Ma is getting married. Only if you agree to that do these things matter."

"Pappu has always been a fool, but you too Apoorva?"

"You people do what you like but I will have no part in this drama. I'll leave tomorrow morning." If there had been a train today, he'd have left today, I think to myself.

"Me too..." so my middle brother will not stay...which left my younger brother and I.

"I'm leaving for my mother's house right now. You stay here and do what you need to, for Ma's marriage. But don't come back to me or the children after that." I know now that he will not stay either. His kids are his weakness because of which he left Ma and went to his wife, in spite of all her taunts and insults...so that meant that only I was left...the play was nearing its climax.

I wear my most serious face and move towards the kitchen, keeping the bubble of laughter contained in my stomach. If I laugh now, it'll shake the whole house and ruin the whole game.

I put my arms around Ma's shoulders as she is making urad puri...Bade Bhaiya's favourite. "Your sons are fools...they couldn't see through their simple mother's wily ways..." I feel like saying.

But Ma is already facing me, her eyes and voice speaking in unison, "I know Appu, even if nobody stands by me, I know you will..."

"Ma, you don't have to put on an act with me also..." I laugh.

"I am not acting...so you are standing by me because you think I'm acting? I've decided and for the first time it is to do with me. And I want to see which of my children will stand by me." Ma's voice is calm and steady...go give this plate to Bade…"

Bhaiya pushes the plate aside. "Just cut out all these gestures. I'm going to a friend's place with my family. I'll take the train tomorrow from there."

Ma has to listen to all this. She doesn't try and stop Bade Bhaiya or pacify him. So does this mean that she is telling the truth?

She will not stop Bade Bhaiya, she knows how wilful he is. But why has Nisha moved right behind Ma, "I don't want to go."

Bade Bhaiya tries to pull her away but she doesn't budge. Then suddenly, he loses patience and his hand moves in the air and lands on his beloved, delicate daughter's face.

Ma's eyes are swimming with tears. A girl who is no longer a child and a father raises his hand… She entreats Nisha to go. Nisha pretends not to see. She moves, not towards the door but to her room where she locks herself in. Bhabhi is crying, "If something happens to my daughter…if she does something foolish in her anger…the shadow of this house is inauspicious."

"She'll do nothing…let her rot. I will not call her…you come…" Bhaiya drags Bhabhi away.

I must take courage from this girl. She has hardly stayed with Ma and yet such unconditional love. Ma has given birth to me and brought me up. On the way, I had thought that I'll give back her lost happiness to Ma and now that I have a chance…?

Is my heart in tune with my mind? My brothers' pain finds a trembling echo in me…my father, hung in a picture, pulses in my heart too. How can Ma give his place to somebody else? We also own that part of her past. Even if she is doing that, why should we? How will we find a father in a stranger's face? My heart too, twists and turns with the hurt I see in my brothers' faces.

I had already thought of the worst, what if Ma had really not been there when I came? I would have slowly made peace with her absence...but then why can't I do the same for her happiness? I rein in my heart firmly.

The phone rings. Nisha picks it up, "Bua...Phoophaji."

"What happened?"

"Nothing."

"Then why did they call you suddenly?"

"Ma is getting married."

"What!"

"Ma is getting married."

"And what are you doing?"

"I'll come only after the marriage Anuj."

"All of you are insane, and what about your brothers? They made such a huge fuss when we were to get married."

"Bhaiya has left."

"Bhaiya has left," repeats Anuj angrily, "And you are staying for her marriage...I respected her so much..."

"You have only respected her, not loved her like a mother..."

"What are you saying...she is like a mother."

"Yes, like a mother, not a mother."

"You have no right to talk to me like that, Apoorva. If you love me, you will return tomorrow."

"Aren't you forgetting something? Our love would have come to nothing, had it not been for Ma. And I love Ma,

Anuj, just like I love you. Perhaps more than you."

Anuj is speechless. And then the dust devils of anger rise again.

"There is no need to come back here after staying for that marriage."

The phone was silent. So was this the limit of Anuj's love, the love that he preened over day and night. How fragile was its thread that it snapped at the first instance of resistance?

I placate myself saying that it was in the heat of the moment. Anuj's tempers are like this and they evaporate soon... My middle brother has dropped off to sleep. We are all in my father's room. Ma has opened her old wooden chest and she is sorting and tidying it. Ma is saying, he is a doctor; he was the one who treated me on the two occasions when I fell. Would we like to meet him... No, then talk to him on the phone? No Ma, if you've chosen him, he must be a good man, or else how could you take such a big decision. Is this evidence of trust in Ma's judgment or a stubborn refusal to let anyone take Pitaji's place? The smells emanating from the chest are very familiar, very personal. A lot like Ma, and this house and Pitaji's memories. I felt I was losing something precious... maikas exist because there is Ma...and she is going. Her eyes are wet too as if in doubt about whether she is doing the right thing. Is Ma also in a dilemma, like every woman, every girl... tense even?

I had also held on to Ma's hand through the night. All that was getting left behind.

Nisha puts her head on Ma's shoulder and I'm

holding on to her wrists. We are no longer women from three generations. We are certainly not grandmother, granddaughter and aunt. We are just three women, three sisters or three friends. Time has removed the barriers around us as it stands mutely in the corner and looks at us. Perhaps it also feels these moments are historic as our silence talks to each other and has so much to say. When did Nisha grow up? We never really knew. When does a woman grow up, who knows?

Ma locks up the room and hands over the keys to me.

"Why me?"

"Just like that...the whole house is lying empty. If she wanted, Chhoti could stay here but I know she will not leave her mother's place. Now even more so...and even if somebody comes, this room will stay locked. I have the keys and now you do too...in case we ever return." Ma says no more.

Nisha is brimming with enthusiasm. She finds bangles for her Dadi and saris in pastel shades. Ma says abashed, "As if all this is suitable at my age?"

The phone rings again, I think it is Anuj, Nisha is on the phone... "Yes, I'll come Papa, just until tomorrow...you send Uncle..."

Will Anuj forgive like Bhaiya? He loves me so much after all?...But Bhaiya is a father and Anuj a husband. I call on his mobile repeatedly, why doesn't he take my calls? I call the landline, "Aunty, this is Rishabh. Uncle is not at home. He's given me the keys; I'm watching the match. Any message for him?"

"Tell him I'm coming back tomorrow. He should come

to the station or else..." My voice catches and I disconnect the phone without completing my sentence. Was Anuj really not there? Was Anuj there?

I tie grains of rice, fresh grass and vermilion in Ma's aanchal with prayers for her happiness. Ma had done the same for me.

Ma has left and we too leave for our destinations.

There is a great tumult in my heart as the train pulls in at the station. I don't have the courage to peep out...what if Anuj is not there...?

The keys Ma gave me jangle in my purse in response... why did she give these to me? Had she understood what was going on...and still...? Will I have to make my way back to that locked room...to her loneliness? Like the sun and moon, had Ma and I exchanged roles?

*Translated by Manisha Chaudhry*

# *Contributors*

**Mannu Bhandari** is one of the most respected names in Hindi writing. A pioneer among women writers, she was associated with the influential post-independence Nai Kahani or 'New Writing' movement in Hindi Literature. Her important works include the novels *Aapka Bunty*, (Yours Bunty) *Mahabhoj*, (The Feast) *Yahi Sach Hai* (This is the Truth) and *Ek Inch Muskaan* (One Inch Smile) co-written with her husband Rajendra Yadav as well as several short story collections. *Mahabhoj* was made into a famous play and *Yahi Sach Hai* into the award-winning film *Rajnigandha*. She has also written many plays and film scripts. Among several others honours she has received the Uttar Pradesh Shalaka Samman and the prestigious Vyas Samman awarded by the K.K. Birla Foundation for her autobiography *Ek Kahani Yeh Bhi* (One More Story) in 2008. Bhandari is considered a path-breaking writer, known for her sensitive and bold portrayal of women in modern Indian society.

**Mamta Kalia** has a master's in English Literature from Delhi University. She writes fiction, poetry, drama, travelogues and essays besides journalistic pieces. Formerly a professor of English, currently she edits *Hindi*, an English language journal of translations. Kalia has more than thirty titles to her credit including her famous novel *Beghar* (Homeless), and her latest *Sukham-Dukham* (Joy-Sorrow). Her poetry collection in English *Tribute to Papa and other Poems* has been included in the curriculum of the Washington State University, Pullman, U.S.A. She has received numerous awards including the U.P. Yashpal Samman for her short story collection *Uska Yauvan* (His Youth) in 1985 and the Kamleshwar Samman in 2007. Plumbing the depths of the human psyche, Kalia examines situations of everyday life with great empathy.

**Mridula Garg** is an eminent Hindi writer who has published in many genres: novels, short stories, drama, essays and travel memoirs. She has 27 books to her credit. Three novels, *Chitta-cobra*, (Country of Goodbyes) *Anitya*, (Halfway to Nowhere) and a short story collection, *Daffodils Jal rahe Hain* (Daffodils on Fire) are available in English. *Miljul Man* is her latest work. Mridula has received many awards including the Vyas Samman for her novel *Kathgulab* (Woodrose) in 2004 and the Hellman-Hammet Grant from The Human Rights Watch, New York. A well-known columnist, she writes a fortnightly column, *Kataksh* (Satire) for *India Today* (Hindi). Freedom is the undercurrent of her work, both for the individual and society.

**RAJEE SETH** is a highly respected name in Hindi writing. A master's in English Literature from Lucknow University, she studied comparative religion and Indian philosophy at the Gujarat Vidyapeeth in Ahmedabad. She is the author of eight collections of short fiction and two novels *Tatsum* and *Nishkavach*, which was translated into English as *Unarmed*. Besides fiction, she has written poetry, critiques and essays. Seth has won many awards, including the Hindi Academy Samman, Anant Kumar Shevade Award and the Bhartiya Bhasha Parishad Award. Her work has been widely translated. She has translated a hundred of Rainer Maria Rilke's letters. Unveiling the turbulence that simmers beneath still facades, her expertly crafted work offers deep insights into the human condition.

**CHANDRAKANTA** hold a master's in Hindi Literature from Pilani, and has published seven novels, fourteen short story collections, collection of poems, essays and memoirs. Her work has been translated into many Indian languages including an English rendering of her novel *Ailan Gali Zinda Hai* (A Street in Srinagar). Chandrakanta has received many awards, among them the Hindi Academy Award and the Vyas Samman for her novel *Katha Satisar*. Noted for her sensitive exploration of the Kashmir problem, Chandrakanta's writing encompasses both socio-economic and political situations, their repercussions on human existence and the plight of the marginalized.

**Chitra Mudgal** is a highly acclaimed Hindi writer and activist. She received her master's in Hindi Literature from SNDT University, Mumbai and became active in social work early in her life. *Aanwa* (Kiln) a classic novel on the trade union movement, is among her best known works. She has two other novels, *Ek Zamin Apni*, *Giligaddu* and several short story collections to her credit as well, besides numerous awards like the Phanishwarnath Renu Award. *Aanwa* received the Vyas Samman in 2006 and has been translated into many languages. Mudgal is still involved with many organizations working for the rights of women and the aged. Her hard hitting, vividly portrayed stories reflect her personal experience and delineate the plight of the underprivileged to powerful effect.

**Alpana Mishra** has won much critical acclaim for her writing during the last decade. A Ph D. in Hindi from Banaras Hindi University, she has published two collections of short stories *Bheetar ka Wakt* (Inner Time) and *Chhawani mein Beghar* (Homeless in the Cantonment). Mishra is at present an Associate Professor of Hindi in Delhi University, and an expert for Braille literature. Many of her short stories and articles have been published in leading magazines and journals. She has received several awards like the Shailesh Matiyani Smriti Samman 2006 from the M.P. Rashtrabhasha Parishad, Bhopal and the Yuva Rachnakar Samman 2008 (Bhartiya Bhasha Parishad, Kolkata). Mishra examines various facets of women's lives with profound understanding. A distinctive style and poetic, beautifully crafted prose marks her writing.

**Manisha Kulshreshtha** is a well-known name among the new generation of women writers in Hindi. With a master's and M. Phil in Hindi, she has three short story collections *Bauni Hoti Parchhai*, (Shrinking Shadows) *Kathputaliyan*, (Puppets) *Kucch bhi to Rumani Nahi* (There's Nothing Romantic) to her credit and a forthcoming novel 'Shigaf'. She contributes to all the leading Hindi journals and also edits the well-known website www.hindinest.com. Kulshreshtha received an award from the Rajasthan Sahitya Academy in 1989 and the Krishna Baldev Vaid Fellowship in 2007. She has translated the work of eminent writers like Borghes and Maya Angelou while her own short stories have been translated into eight languages. Her finely wrought stories explore many facets of human existence.

**Pratyaksha** is well-known for her highly evocative, experimental stories among the younger generation of Hindi writers. A master's in history and an MBA in finance, she started writing stories and poems in 2006. Presently the Chief Manager Finance in the Powergrid Corporation of India Ltd., her stories, poems, travelogues and book reviews have been published in leading Hindi literary magazines. Bhartiya Gyanpeeth published a collection of her stories titled *Jungle ka Jadoo Til Til* in 2008. Right now she is working on a second book of stories, a book of her blog collections and a novel in English. Pratyaksha's work is remarkable for her ingenious use of language to create mood and atmosphere and her innovative choice of themes and topics.

**KAVITA** made her mark on the Hindi writing scene at a relatively young age. A master's in Hindi Literature from the Bhimarao Ambedkar Bihar University, Bihar, she has two collections, *Mere Naap ke Kapde* (Clothes Made to my Measure) and *Ulatbaansi* (Transformation) published, with a third collection *Patthar Maati, Dhoop* (Rock, Earth and Sunshine) and a novel *Lautati Dishayein* (Recoiling Winds) forthcoming. She has also edited and compiled a collection of essays *Main Hans Nahi Padhta* (I Don't Read the Magazine Hans) and well-known author and editor Rajendra Yadav's correspondence with the authors Mohan Rakesh, Kamleshwar and critic Naamwar Singh under the title *Ab ve Yahan Nahi Rehte* (They Don't Live Here Any More). Kavita addresses provocative issues that challenge the establishment in a direct, straightforward style.

**VANDANA RAG** is another of the exciting new voices in Hindi. A master's in History from Delhi University, *Utopia,* her short story collection was recently published by Rajkamal Prakashan. Rag contributes regularly to literary journals and has translated E. J. Hobsbawm's classic *The Age of Capital* from English to Hindi for Samvaad Prakashan. Cinema is another of her special interests and she has worked in a few short films. Currently she is writing a book based on the cultural traditions of Bhopal in English. Vandana's stories express powerful realistic images and question the injustices and paradoxes prevalent in society and the human mind.

## Translators

**Madhu B. Joshi** was educated in New Delhi. Poet, translator, editor, her wide range of interests includes education and media. National Book Trust and Rajkamal Prakashan have published her books for children.

**Raji Narasimhan** is basically a fiction-writer. Her second novel, *Forever Free,* was prescribed in the English course of IIT, Delhi, in the 1980s. She has done a considerable amount of translation work as well, mostly from Hindi to English. Her translations include *Unarmed*, a rendering of Rajee Seth's novella *Nishkavach*, brought out by Macmillan in 1998. In 2006 her translation if Maitreyi Pushpa's novel, *Alma Kabutari* was published by Katha. It was short-listed for the Vodafone Crossword Award for Translation in 2008.

**Prem Kumari Srivastava** is Associate Professor of English at Maharaja Agrasen College and currently Fellow, Institute of Lifelong Learning, University of Delhi, India. She is presently engaged in web-based course content creation and research on 'English language learning' and 'cultural diversity' in India. She has presented/published several Research Papers/Chapters in National and International Conferences/ Seminars and Journals/Books in areas such as women's studies, popular culture, translation (Hindi to English), bhakti consciousness, oral narratives and literary adaptations in Cinema. She also writes and publishes poetry.

**Gitanjali Chawla** is an assistant professor in the Department of English, University of Delhi, currently teaching in Maharaja Agrasen College. She has been teaching English Literature since 1994 and has taught in various University Colleges. She is also a teaching faculty member of the Department of Journalism and specializes in traditional folk media.

**Anu Jaidev** teaches English Literature at Maharaja Agrasen College. She is a poet and translator. Her poems have appeared in Sahitya Akademi's literary journal *Indian Literature* and she also translates texts from Hindi to English.

**Vibha S. Chauhan**, Reader at the Department of English, Zakir Husain College, University of Delhi has co-authored *Maa – Siddheshwari*, a biography of the renowned thumri singer. She is co-editor of *Cultural Diversity, Linguistic Plurality and Literary Tradition in India*, now an undergraduate text at the University of Delhi. Her Hindi novel *Ganga Jamuna Beech* published by Alekh Prakashan received wide acclaim. She has also translated Joginder Paul's Urdu novel *Paar Pare* into English as *Beyond Black Waters*. Her English poems have appeared in collections like *Temba Tupu: Walking Naked* and *Confluence*. Chauhan's major research and publications focus on the cultures, languages and the exclusion of non-urban and socio-economically marginalized communities like the adivasis and Dalits in India.